Let's Walk

Mark Linley

Meridian Books

Published 1988 by Meridian Books.

©Mark Linley 1988

British Library Cataloguing in Publication Data

Linley, Mark
    Let's Walk.
    1. Recreations : Walking–Manuals
    I. Title
    796.5'1

    ISBN 1-869922-03-4

Typeset from AppleWorks discs by Minstrel, Dane Road, Sale, Cheshire.
Cover design by Technographic Design & Print Ltd., Saxmundham, Suffolk.
Printed in Great Britain by A. Wheaton & Co. Ltd., Exeter.

Meridian Books, 40 Hadzor Road, Oldbury, Warley, West Midlands B68 9LA.

Contents

Introduction
Why Walk?

Why walk when you can drive, be driven or be carried? Why go for rambles when you can lie about in a contented heap? Must you venture out into awful weather when you can watch the storm clouds from a cosy well-worn armchair? Why move about when you can enjoy the sunshine from the depth of a sagging deck-chair in your back garden?

Well, no, you don't have to do any of these. But although you may be fit enough to pull a pint, push a pen or a steam iron, chop chips or hide from your in-laws, none of these activities will do much for your health, especially your power unit, the heart, or your built-in computer, the brain. But walking, especially in the delightful British countryside, can induce a feeling of joy and an awakening of the spirit of adventure. The sight of trees, hills and rivers, rather than high rise flats and factories, can refresh the eyes and the system. The change from petrol fumes to clean, sweet air can work wonders for your sense of well-being. At first,

1

walking over the hills may make you breathless, but you will soon find that you can manage quite tough climbs without running the risk of making early use of your life insurance policy. Getting really fit can change your appearance, improve your complexion and stimulate your mind. Your friends will hardly recognise you from the ashen-faced, gasping wreck that was formerly you.

Rain, if it isn't the acid sort, can be a tonic for your skin. A trudge through a mini-monsoon has its blessings, and ploughing your way through deep snow will do wonders for your circulation. The stresses of modern life will tend to diminish when you set out on a walk, and are usually quite forgotten by the end — in fact, you might feel quite human.

Becoming fit and staying that way is fun. You will be able to trot upstairs — and still have breath to talk to the cat at the top. Instead of thrashing about all night like a stranded whale you will enjoy deep refreshing sleep. You won't be out of puff after running for the bus. Fitness is health, can be fun, and the path to a vital ripe old age.

Walking is one of the simplest of exercises and is one that is open to all who have mobile legs and a desire to move them. Of course, it's wise to start off gradually and build up, particularly if you are over forty and have not been in the habit of walking. If you seldom go further than to or from your car, local pub or betting shop don't be tempted to dash off on a 250 mile trek up the Pennine Way, at least not without first making your will and taking a stretcher party along with you!

To start, try a short distance each day, one or two miles if you can. Think about leaving your car at home, and walk to the railway station or bus stop. As well as doing wonders for your blood pressure it will get you to work in a better mood and in a more relaxed state of mind. Don't use the lift; walk, or trot gently, up the stairs.

Walking in built up areas need not be a bore if you develop an interest in architecture or local history. Hours of enjoyment can be obtained by getting an old map and exploring to see how your area has changed in the last hundred years or so. Reprints of the first series of Ordnance Survey maps, dating back to the early part of the last century, are available from bookshops and these can be fascinating sources of information — while at the same time helping you to get your lungs and legs in working order. You might even feel inspired to write a book on your discoveries and help you (or your publisher) to make a fortune.

Think about how much you spend each year in keeping your car in working order, then consider what you could do to keep that priceless asset, your body, in good trim. Remember, you can't trade that in for this year's new model. Looking after it will damage your bank balance less than your car will.

2

Ramble, or amble, at your own speed and gradually increase the distances covered. With a little practice you should easily be able to manage five or six miles, and two or three times this distance when your newly discovered muscles are tuned up and your heart and lungs are running smoothly.

If you have children, regular walking from an early age will encourage them towards a healthier life style. Walking holidays with them can be much more interesting and provide far more mental stimulation than always sitting about on a polluted and overcrowded beach.

Well, if you have read this far, congratulations! — you are probably going to become one of us — the great rambling mob. Now read on to acquire and develop the skills that you need to enjoy walking to the full.

1

Companions

If you are a confirmed loner and are completely happy in your own company maybe this chapter won't interest you. But even so, you might find that the company of others has, at times, its attractions, perhaps because transport is a problem or because you want to go into the mountains where solo walking could be a bit risky.

You can usually be assured of a friendly welcome if you join a walking group. There are lots of these around, especially in the big towns, where a wonderful family spirit prevails. Your local library should be able to put you in touch with your nearest group, and camping and outdoor shops will also be good sources of information. There is a list of useful addresses at the end of the book.

Groups vary considerably in the type of walk that they arrange. Some are hill and mountain walking groups that like to go in for the tough stuff! Others have more modest ambitions and may simply cater for the retired or those who want nothing more strenuous than an afternoon or evening stroll. Some of the larger groups cater for a range of levels and will have two or more parties of different grades of walking difficulty. The A-party might do fourteen or more miles on an average walk, the B-party might do eight to ten miles, the C-party four or five. Sometimes there might be an A+ walk for the really energetic.

An advantage of a large group is that it can hire a coach to take its members out on their rambles and bring them back at the end of the day. Smaller groups will make use of public transport or private cars, the motorists giving lifts to the non-motorists. Coach travel does make life very much easier, and tired walkers are not faced with a possibly long drive after their outing. More distant rambles can be organised, and the route does not have to be circular — which is usually necessary with a car ramble.

4

Don't be put off by the thought of a full day's walk of, perhaps, six or seven hours. There will be stops for drinks, lunch, loo, and for admiring the view. A-parties may walk about three miles an hour, B and C-parties rather less and, of course, have shorter walks with more stops and time for looking around. The rate of progress will be slower on the hills and mountains, perhaps an hour for every 2000 feet climbed depending on the nature of the terrain.

If you join a group, always find out on the first few rambles the distances and degrees of difficulty involved (if there is a choice of A, B or C-walks). Don't start by taking on too difficult a walk — it may discourage you and hold back the rest of the party. After two or three walks you will find which party suits you best.

THE RAMBLERS' ASSOCIATION

The nationwide Ramblers' Association has area and local groups all over the country. For over fifty years the RA has campaigned for walkers, and has done a tremendous amount of good work. It fights all threats to the countryside and helps members and non-members alike to walk wherever there are rights of way.

The RA continually battles against the loss of footpaths and for their maintenance and protection. The cost of this is, of course, high and the biggest part of the RA's income comes from subscriptions and voluntary donations. The annual subscription is quite modest and brings many benefits to members.

Members receive an excellent bi-monthly magazine, *The Rambler*, which carries news items and features on various aspects of walking, all of interest to everyone with a love of the countryside. They also receive an annual accommodation guide, invaluable to anyone planning a walking holiday.

Maps can be borrowed from the RA library, and the national office will give advice, and provide leaflets, on various aspects of rambling. A number of outdoor shops will give RA members a discount on purchases.

All RA groups have experienced members whose wealth of knowledge can be called upon whenever help or advice is needed. Many big cities have their own RA groups. My own, for example, is very well organised with a comprehensive programme of Sunday rambles, all carefully planned months in advance. It also has several social events during the year: these include interesting talks, slide shows and cheese and wine evenings. Easter and August Bank Holiday long weekends are arranged in attractive walking areas such as Exmoor, Snowdonia, North Yorkshire and other great places, with accommodation in youth hostels and guest houses. These provide excellent opportunities for members to get to know each other better.

Members of my group cover a wide cross section of the community and include managers, doctors, postmen, teachers, drivers, clerks, engineers, unemployed (alas), a mad artist and even a book publisher. There is a wide age distribution within the group, and walking parties often range from teens (and sometimes younger) to the 60+.

OTHER GROUPS

The growing popularity of walking means that a growing number of rambling holidays are being offered by a variety of organisations. Two of the oldest of these are the COUNTRYWIDE HOLIDAYS ASSOCIATION (CHA) and HF HOLIDAYS.

The CHA is a long established walking and activity holiday organisation with fourteen country houses and coastal hotels. Holidays are characterised by a house party atmosphere with daily walks and evening socials. Each centre offers a choice of graded walks led by experienced guides. Centres, also, are graded according to the type of walks provided which range from the very strenuous to the gentle. The Association also arranges walking and activity holidays abroad.

HF HOLIDAYS, which has twenty-two centres in Britain, is a similar organisation to CHA. It also provides holidays abroad.

Both of these organisations run local walking groups offering regular Sunday rambles and, sometimes, mid-week rambles for the retired and those without jobs. Socials and other events are held regularly.

SMALL BANDS

If you live far from a town or city and cannot, or prefer not to, join a rambling group you could form a small private group for local walking. There must be hundreds of such bands, made up of friends, neighbours, workmates or colleagues, scattered around the country. Walks further afield can be arranged by using public transport or cars.

Car rambles do not necessarily have to be circular if two or more cars are involved. First drive to the *finishing* point, leave one or more cars there, then transport everyone to the *start* of the walk leaving the remaining cars there. After the walk repeat the process in reverse, driving back to the start to pick up the rest of the cars. If this procedure is not to collapse in chaos all the drivers must be carefully briefed as to the location of the starting and finishing points and the route between them!

Small parties can move about faster than a large group and so have a bit more freedom to explore, side-track, or change plans fast. One drawback to a big party is that members can become strung out on the ramble, especially if there are a lot of stiles, fences or difficult ground to get across.

6

Publicans normally welcome thirsty ramblers but, especially in a small pub, excessively large groups are likely to overwhelm the regulars and be somewhat less popular.

For ideas on where to walk consult your bookshop or library. There is now a multitude of guidebooks which describe walks — some cover the whole of the country, others are very local. Many are published by small local publishers, some by rambling groups themselves. The Ramblers' Association produces a series of fact sheets, free to its members, covering most of the British counties and listing walks guides for those counties. You will find more suggestions on choosing where to go in chapter 4.

WHO TO AVOID

Before going out on a group ramble be sure that you know how tough or otherwise the walk is going to be. Avoid SAS type groups if all you want is a gentle stroll. Equally, don't underestimate your capabilities. Something too easy can cause frustration and make you an irritating companion to those who don't have your amount of energy.

Don't go out with untrained or unruly dogs. Man's best friend can quickly become man's best fiend when let loose in the countryside! Farmers have the right to shoot on sight any dog that is seen chasing or molesting sheep, cattle or stock. Sometimes the best behaved pet dog will go beserk when it sees running farm animals. If you are not sure about your dog either keep it on a lead, or make it stay at home with a case of dogfood for company. If you are walking with a group you may not be allowed to take a dog, especially if it is a coach ramble.

Avoid going by yourself unless you are really confident of your capabilities. Certainly there are pleasures in walking alone, but there are also dangers. Mountains look beautiful on a nice sunny day but can quite suddenly become hazardous to the lone walker. Mountain Rescue Teams help or save many people who think that they can walk up or down mountains. Some of those rescued are intelligent folk who have courage but little know-how. They are often caught out on their own with no equipment, are unsuitably dressed, and have no food, drink, map, compass or survival gear. Their intentions may be good but they lack experience and can be a danger not only to themselves but also to those who go out to find them. There is safety in numbers and ramblers in groups can look out for each other, share knowledge and pool equipment, etc. if necessary.

2
Clothes. Trendy or Trampy?

Walking need not be an expensive activity, but there are certain essential items which must be purchased. In addition to seeking advice from fellow walkers try to find a camping/outdoor shop which has staff experienced in outdoor activities. You will benefit from talking with them.

You will find these shops in the larger towns, and often in smaller places in the popular walking areas like the Lake District and Snowdonia. Most chain stores carry a selection of good outdoor gear as do mail order companies.

Walking magazines regularly carry reviews of walking gear and these can be a useful source of information. It is a good idea for the beginner to get a mail order catalogue from one of the many companies that sell by post. It will provide a good introduction to what is available.

THE BASICS

When you first go into an outdoor shop you will be amazed at the amount of equipment on show, but to start with it is not necessary to spend a lot to obtain the main essentials, which are boots and waterproofs.

You will also need a rucksack or something in which to carry your food and gear, and the correct clothes for the time of year; thermals for winter and

9

cotton for high summer. Don't be coy about wearing 'Long Johns' or long-sleeved reach-me-down vests. These useful garments are ideal for the winter months. The principle is to dress so that you will be dry and comfortable whatever the conditions.

SWEATERS

It is wise to have one or more pure wool sweaters. Even on the hottest days it can be mighty cold high up in the hills or on the moors, especially so when you stop for a drink, a rest, or to get your wind back. Some pullovers are proofed to keep out the wet but still to let out body moisture. When you go out, always have an extra pullover or sweater with you. Two or more thin woollen sweaters will conserve more heat than a single thick one.

COATS AND JACKETS

There are now so many different sorts of walking coat that it is difficult to know what to buy. The main thing is to ensure that it is windproof and has a good hood. Wind has a considerable cooling effect on the body and needs to be protected against. Some people prefer to walk in sweaters with just a thin windproof jacket. Others will wear a quilted jacket; others still (if they can afford it) prefer the jacket to have a waterproof outer covering as well. The latter can cost up to around £200 so don't get carried away before you have had plenty of walking experience!

Top quality coats are made from specially constructed material which keeps out the rain, but allows body moisture to escape, thus reducing or eliminating condensation of perspiration. This can be a boon when the weather is both wet and warm, or when climbing produces a lot of body heat. Cheaper coats may be waterproof but do not have this property, so you can end up very wet, just from your body moisture.

All good walking jackets should have plenty of pockets which are either zipped or will fasten down to keep out the wet. Waterproof coats usually have a hood attached to the collar, and these are very handy for wet days, or when it is cold. Some hoods are detachable or will fold into a zipped compartment in the collar.

There are good woollen blousons for winter use and lightweight ones for summer. But look for plenty of pockets — ramblers tend to carry lots of bits and pieces.

A typical rambling group will usually display both today's fashions in walking clothes and those of past years. Most people are only too happy to talk about their choice of clothes, but sometimes tend to think that theirs is the best around — not always of great help to the newcomer. The Ramblers' Association magazine, *The Rambler*, has frequent useful articles on new clothes and materials, and this can be very helpful when you are deciding what to buy.

TROUSERS

Well made, sturdy trousers are a must. These will have a lot of wear so it is wise to get the best — wool for winter and maybe, if it's warm, a man-made fabric for summer. All outdoor shops have a good range.

Breeches (or striders as they are often called) are very comfortable if well made and properly fitting. Some have double knees and seats and come in a variety of weights and textures. Pockets are usually zipped or buttoned.

A good pair of breeches can last a long time. I have worn the same wind, thorn and shower proof breeches for ten years and they should last for many more.

Breeches need knee-length socks to go with them. On warm days these can be turned down for coolness.

Denims or jeans should not be worn unless you are quite sure of good weather. This material does not keep out the wind, cold or wet and if conditions turn bad this can have unpleasant consequences with a real risk of hypothermia.

11

SHORTS

When it is sunny many ramblers are tempted to rush out in shorts. While this may delight their companions the wearers can easily collect nettle and insect stings. The weather can change fast and catch most of us out at some time or other. If the going is through bramble, thorn scrub, nettles or gorse then shorts will not be of much use. But if the walk is through gentle meadows, or along a seashore, shorts would be great. It is advisable to carry trousers or breeches in your rucksack in case the weather or the going turns tough.

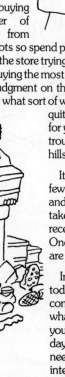

The same comments, of course, also apply to skirts.

BOOTS

Always take great care when buying boots. The greatest number of problems in walking result from uncomfortable or badly fitting boots so spend plenty of time making your purchase, and don't be afraid to pad around the store trying lots of pairs before deciding. A slick salesperson might con you into buying the most expensive boots known, but you are the only one who can make a judgment on their comfort and how they suit you. Explain clearly to the salesperson what sort of walking you want the boots for. Make quite sure that there is adequate space for your toes: if not you are likely to be in trouble, especially when descending hills.

It is a good idea also to wear them a few times at home — and try walkng up and down stairs. Any good shop will take boots back on production of the receipt provided they are not marked. Once you have done a day's walking you are stuck with them.

In the past, boots were very heavy but today the fashion has changed considerably. To start, you must decide what sort of walking you intend to do. If you confine your outings to summer days and good weather you will only need fairly lightweight boots. But if you intend to walk all year round and in all weathers then a heavier boot is necessary. If you propose to undertake tough mountain walking in snow conditions using crampons and an ice axe then a heavy boot with a hinged sole is required.

Boots that will cope with any sort of terrain and most weather conditions should have one-piece leather uppers and thick moulded hard rubber soles. A good weather-proof tongue is important: this can be a weak point in keeping out the wet. But no boots are ever totally waterproof — water will eventually go through the stitching holes if you are walking all day in wet grass or waterlogged ground. However, a good pair of boots is the best investment that you can make if you want to enjoy your walking.

With heavy boots allow sufficient room in them for two pairs of socks, a thin pair under a thicker pair for foot comfort. This means that you will need to choose a half or whole size bigger than you wear in shoes. It is a good idea to take your walking socks with you when you go to buy buy boots — but the staff in any good outdoor shop will lend you a pair if you don't have your own. With lighter boots a single pair of socks may be adequate.

Always break in boots before using them for serious walking. Although modern boots are easier to become accustomed to than those of a few years ago, never embark on a walk of any length in new boots. Well designed boots might appear to fit perfectly, but many people have slight imperfections in their feet to which new footwear has to mould itself. So start off with some short walks in your neighbourhood, then try something a bit longer until you are quite sure that all is well. Some walkers soak new boots in water, then wear them damp to allow the leather to adapt to the contours of their feet.

To keep leather supple and waterproof, boots need to be kept clean and periodically treated with wax, grease or oil. There are various proprietary types available and the outdoor shop where you buy your boots should be able to advise you. After a ramble always wash off the mud as soon as you can. Don't use oil or grease too frequently as this can make the leather too soft and destroy its waterproofing. Always go by the manufacturer's instructions.

Never dry boots too quickly by putting them near a fire or radiator, or in an airing cupboard. This will cause the leather to crack.

Admittedly, some walkers do go out in trainer shoes. But these give no ankle support and provide little protection against water and mud. They give little grip on slippery or rock surfaces or when going downhill. So think carefully if you are tempted to economise on footwear.

Lightweight fell boots are much cheaper and easier to adapt to than walking boots. They can be very comfortable, especially if you find heavier boots something of a burden. But if you buy them make sure that they have a substantial sole, and remember that they may not be suitable for very wet conditions.

SOCKS

Wearing the right socks for walking is most important. It is usual to wear two pairs, one thin inner pair and one thick pair on top of these. Woollen socks are best for rambling. Wool has natural insulation and moisture absorbing qualities, and helps to prevent you getting too hot (as any sheep will tell you). It doesn't feel cold and clammy when wet from rain, or if you sweat: man-made materials are not so good in this respect.

Always wear the right size of sock. Socks which are too short or too long or have awkward seams can cause soreness or blisters and may, if worn regularly, lead to long term foot complaints. No matter what kind of boots you use, if the socks are wrong you will never feel comfortable when walking.

Cushion loop socks can be recommended — but there are now many kinds of first class socks on the market and your outdoor shop will advise you. Waterproof socks are now available. They are quite expensive but very useful if you can't rely on your boots keeping out the wet.

SHIRTS

Woollen shirts for winter are a sound idea, with cotton for summer and, perhaps, short sleeves depending on the weather. Tee shirts can be good for hot days, but avoid nylon as this material gives no protection against sunburn. There are now many good synthetic materials used for walking shirts.

WATERPROOFS

Sound waterproof clothes are a must when you ramble in Britain. Even on the most promising day it can, as we all know, suddenly change and pour down with rain. The number of days in a year when it throws it down non-stop is actually quite small, but even a half-hour's blitz can leave you pretty sodden and cold.

Waterproofs come in both lightweight and heavyweight strengths, and can be one piece or two piece. One piece is the knee length 'cagoule' which may or may not have a zipped opening front. The opening front is probably better, provided that rain cannot penetrate the zip, because you can partly open it for ventilation purposes in the intervals between showers.

More commonly met today is the two piece hip length waterproof jacket worn with waterproof overtrousers. As described above, the more expensive jackets are themselves waterproof and some walkers wear these as standard. Overtrousers, as the name suggests, are worn over trousers or breeches. To avoid having to remove your boots when putting them on, overtrousers usually have zipped or Velcro openings at the bottom of the legs.

The main problem with waterproofs is condensation of perspiration which on a strenuous walk, or one in hot weather, can make you very wet indeed. Modern materials can reduce this by a considerable extent but good ventilation is a great help. So open up zips when the rain eases and let the air circulate through your waterproofs as much as you can.

Waterproof hoods, which are an integral part of most waterproof jackets, are fine but wearing them does seem to add to condensation problems. A reasonably waterproof hat might be found preferable provided the weather is not too dreadful.

GAITERS

An alternative to waterproof overtrousers is gaiters. Some pull on over boots and legs, others zip down the sides and hook onto the boots. They are made of similar

14

material to waterproofs, or of canvas. They are very useful, not only for keeping out the wet, but for protecting the legs against thorns, brambles and mud. They also help to protect the upper part of the foot which they cover. Some ramblers wear them as standard, leaving them off only on the hottest days.

You can also buy anklets which zip up the side and will keep mud and stones out of your boots. They can be worn throughout the year.

Modern gaiters and anklets weigh very little and are no trouble to pop into your rucksack. After use they are easily washed and dried.

HATS

Hats are useful for keeping body heat in. On a cold day 40 per cent of body heat can escape through the top of your head. Hats with brims can be tricky in wind, and many a rambler has watched headgear sail off into the sky. The best bet is a woollen balaclava, the sort loved by bank robbers. The Russian type, made of simulated fur, is good for very cold days, and has pull down ear muffs built in.

For hot days and direct sunshine a light hat is a great aid, especially if you are rather thin on top. As well as protecting you against the sun it is also useful for keeping insects at bay, especially midges which seem to like scalps for tea.

GLOVES

Mitts or warm gloves are needed in cold weather, and quite often when tackling mountain climbs. If your hands are cold you generally feel cold all over, and miserable with it.

Wool is best for gloves, but you can also buy thermal ones which are good. Mitts can be lined with sheep's wool and these are probably the warmest for the winter. For high mountain walks there are the

15

double lined sort as used in Everest expeditions. A good idea in really cold weather is to wear thermal gloves with mitts over the top.

Waterproof gloves are necessary if you are out in really bad weather. A useful substitute is a pair of thin rubber gloves of the household kind which can be pulled over your ordinary gloves to make them waterproof.

You can also buy hand warmers; some of these use charcoal, others rely on chemicals. If you use them be sure to follow the maker's directions — a fire in your pocket could have nasty consequences!

EX-ARMY GEAR

Most of the types of clothing mentioned above can be bought from ex-army stores, and this includes boots. While some of it is unsuitable much can be used by walkers. You can find very well made coats, jackets and trousers which won't be as expensive as purpose made rambling gear. But be sure that you understand what you want — you won't get the professional advice that you expect from a good outdoor shop.

If you fancy yourself as a Red Devil or a Marine Commando have a look at this gear. You could surprise your fellow walkers!

3

What to Carry

Some ramblers like to take with them everything that they are likely to need in all weather conditions. Others prefer to travel light. You have a choice but there are three absolute essentials:

1. Food to sustain you on the ramble,
2. Enough to drink,
3. Waterproofs to keep you dry and warm,

plus, of course, something to carry all this in.

RUCKSACK

You will need a good rucksack for rambles. Many walkers have two — a small one for day walks and a larger one for walking holidays. Rucksacks come in many sizes, shapes and colours and most outdoor shops will provide a somewhat bewildering choice.

Some people think it better to buy a rucksack that is on the big size rather than one that is too small. We tend to add to our gear as we get more involved in rambling — and, of course, there might be the choice of picking up a Tang Dynasty vase from a village bazaar, or you might want to take back a priceless gift for your in-laws. However, another school of thought is not to buy one that is too big, for if you do you will inevitably tend to fill it with unnecessary weight. Remember that on a strenuous walk every ounce can count.

Small rucksacks can be quite cheap — just a few pounds — but you might consider a more costly one with padded shoulder straps, several pockets and a lightweight frame which will keep a filled rucksack away from your body to avoid a sweaty back.

A good larger rucksack should have a strong waist-belt which will take most of the weight away from your shoulders — a great aid if you are carrying everything with you on a walking holiday.

The capacity of rucksacks is usually measured in litres. For day walking 25 litres should be very adequate; for holidays aim for a minimum of 55 litres.

Although rucksacks are often claimed to be waterproof it is wise not to rely on this. One or two plastic bags will keep clothes and food dry. Outdoor shops sell rucksack liners made of stout plastic which will keep everything dry even in the wettest of conditions. A large bin liner will be better than nothing. Even so it is still a useful tip to keep various items in separate plastic bags. These make things much easier to find, particularly desirable if you are carrying everything with you on a week's walking holiday. A plastic bag or bin liner is useful to have with you to spread out on damp ground when you want to sit down.

It pays to take a bit of care in packing your rucksack. Keep hard or angular objects, such as sandwich boxes or thermos flasks, away from your body so that they don't dig into your back. Have your waterproofs on top for easy reach. Remember to fasten all pockets, and if there is a draw string pull this tight. Many a walker has smashed a thermos by forgetting to do this — the author three times!

In a large rucksack pack heavy items towards the top and close to the body. This will help to keep you better balanced.

FOOD

If your ramble includes a stop at a coffee shop and a pub lunch you may not need to take food, though it is sensible to always have something in your rucksack for emergencies. But walks off the beaten track mean that you are responsible for your own requirements so work out how much it will take to keep you going.

Sandwiches of wholemeal bread with polyunsaturated margarine and filled with cottage, or other low fat, cheese are healthy and nourishing. Fresh tomatoes, celery sticks, lettuce and fruit are all great for sustaining you on a hard walk. Nuts and raisins are a useful food and have a high protein content. Dried dates also, as any Bedouin will tell you, are very sustaining.

Cold potatoes are nice to eat on a cold day and give fast energy, as do most starchy foods. Kendal Mint Cake is popular with some ramblers and climbers and, like chocolate bars and biscuits, is another fast energy giver. But remember that these items contain a lot of sugar.

A plastic box will help to prevent sandwiches from getting flattened. Old ice cream or margarine containers are ideal for this purpose and are also excellent for salads.

Don't overdo things at the lunch stop — an overfull stomach can spoil the pleasure of the afternoon, and is not the best preparation for a steep climb.

DRINKS

Even when walking in wintry conditions your body will use up some of its liquid supply, and the harder the going the more you will dehydrate. On hot days you will need far more to drink than on cold days and it is wiser to take too much rather than too little. Thirst is distressing and debilitating.

A thermos flask of tea or coffee is ideal for a mid-morning or afternoon break. Packs of pure fruit juices are excellent and much more refreshing than fruit squashes containing additives and sweeteners. A can of beer or lager is fine if you like a tipple. Probably best of all, when you are really thirsty, is plain water. You may prefer natural spring water, now readily available from supermarkets, to the chlorinated product which comes out of the tap. Outdoor shops sell a good range of bottles for carrying water.

A drink of cool fresh water from a mountain stream is one of the delights of high walking. However, make sure, before you do this, that you are well away from sheep country or you might find that the water has been contaminated with something nasty! If in doubt about possible pollution — don't! A tube of water sterilizing tablets for emergencies is a useful addition to your rucksack.

WATERPROOFS

We described these in the last chapter. Don't go without them unless you are really sure of the weather. Never leave them behind when you are in the mountains. Even if it is not wet they can provide extra warmth in an emergency.

EXTRA CLOTHING

Always have something extra with you. A hat and gloves don't take up much room and in the UK are worth keeping with you for most of the year. A spare sweater is strongly recommended and spare socks if you can't rely on your boots being waterproof.

MAPS AND COMPASS

If you are walking with a group your leader should carry these. Nevertheless if you have your own they can add a lot of interest to your walk. More about them in chapters 7 and 8. A plastic map case will allow you to hang your map round your neck and will keep it dry in bad weather.

Some ramblers like to know exactly how far they have walked and take to carrying pedometers. These are small clock-like devices that record distances walked in miles and kilometres after setting them to your accurately measured average pace. Alternatively you can buy map measures with which you can trace out your route on the map and then read off the distance involved. These are particularly useful when planning a walk.

A simple way of calculating your mileage is to just multiply the hours walked by two. This will give you a fair idea of the number of miles covered: two miles per hour is a reasonably average pace for a day's walking over a variety of terrains.

NOTEBOOK

A notebook with pen or pencil will often come in handy. You might like to keep a note of where you have been, how far, with whom and interesting things you have seen. There is something new to see, experience and enjoy on every ramble and a record will enable you to recall and savour past pleasures.

TORCH

Always have a torch with you on winter walks or if there is any chance that you will still be walking when it is dark. As well as helping you to pick out your way it is mighty useful to have a torch to examine maps when it is getting dark or is foggy. Choose one that gives a good beam and is light. Check the battery regularly and replace it at least every two years even if you have not used it. To avoid a torch getting switched on by accident in your rucksack turn the batteries round inside the case.

SURVIVAL BAG

One of the many materials to come out of space exploration is a sort of foil with wonderful insulation properties. Very lightweight survival bags are made from this and will fold away into small pockets. Most outdoor shops have them. They are invaluable in an emergency and will keep someone warm who may be injured or suffering from hypothermia until help can be obtained. Check them regularly as they tend to deteriorate after a time.

BINOCULARS

These are useful on most walks. You can study wildlife, birds in particular, and use them in conjunction with your map to help plot routes or discover exactly where you are. The only drawback that they might have is weight: small, lightweight binoculars are on sale but they are costly. Binoculars need looking after and are not the most robust of instruments for carrying about. They can go out of adjustment if knocked, dropped or handled roughly.

FIRST AID

Always go prepared for minor emergencies such as bites, cuts and blisters. Brambles, barbed wire and insects are common hazards in the countryside. A tube of antiseptic cream is handy for scratches and cuts. Band Aids, or similar adhesive dressings will deal with cuts and blisters and should be carried in a variety of sizes. Moleskin adhesive dressing is particularly useful for blisters. A tube of antihistamine cream is valuable for the more unpleasant bites and stings. It is a wise precaution to have regular anti-tetanus injections — your GP will provide these and advise you on how often you should have a repeat.

If you are the sort of person who is regarded as a free meal by the insect population take along a tube of insect repellent. A hat will keep the little perishers from nibbling your scalp. Be warned that midges are especially active in Scotland in the summer months.

WALKING STICK

Walking sticks, once very fashionable, are not seen so often these days but can be very useful on rambles. A stick can be used for testing boggy ground and so avoiding getting stuck. It will also fend off thorn branches, brambles and undergrowth. One with a pointed ferrule is especially handy on hills and mountains or wherever the terrain is difficult.

Folding sticks are now available and can be kept in your rucksack, then brought out when conditions demand.

FINALLY...

To remind yourself of everything that you are going to need when you go walking make a list of i) essential items and ii) items for special occasions. Then keep this handy in your rucksack. But be realistic in your choices. Remember that you will have to carry them all on your back!

4

Where to go?

When you trundle off into the great outdoors remember that all land is owned by someone, and not all landowners want your size ten boots crashing over their pastures. You have your rights, however, and can visit much of England and Wales on 120,000 miles of public footpaths, byways and bridleways. You also have the right of access to much open country which may be areas of mountain, moor, down, heath, cliff, seashore or beach. Local Authorities make access agreements or orders allowing the public a legal right to go on foot (usually) in these areas.

In Scotland the law of public access is rather different and rights of way are not shown on maps in red or green as they are in England and Wales. But you can normally use paths and tracks shown on the maps in black, though some paths may be closed in the grouse shooting season.

In other places access may be by invitation of the landowner, for example, the Forestry Commission or National Trust. If you are not a member of the Trust you may have to pay a small entrance fee to go on their property.

On some land used by the Ministry of Defence walking may be restricted on certain days of the year.

UP AND DOWN THE HIGHWAY

A highway that can be used only for walking is called a footpath (surprise!). If a track is also used for cycling, or riding or leading a horse on, it is termed a bridleway and will be wider than a footpath and a mighty lot muddier in wet weather — the horses having churned it up.

A byway is often an old road used mainly by the public for walking and riding but is open to traffic as a legal right. You may hear about highways called RUPPs. Rupps are not some exotic sort of Swedish walking boots but Roads Used as Public Paths. Rights on these are so messy that they are being reclassified under other headings — footpaths, byways or bridleways. This should make things easier for ramblers.

You can gain access to some land by tradition regardless of whether the landowner agrees or not, but all access should be checked before venturing into the

23

unknown. Ordnance Survey maps show public rights of way in green on the 1:25,000 scale (Pathfinder) maps, and in red on the 1:50,000 (Landranger) maps.

The good old National Trust provides public access to miles of coastline and countryside which they own. These areas are usually outstandingly beautiful and many people benefit from the Trust's investments. Should you join this worthy organisation your subscription will help their cause and allow you free admission to their numerous parks, lands and buildings. They own many stately homes and places of historic interest.

WAYMARKING

As you ramble along your chosen path you will sometimes see small coloured arrows on trees, fences and posts. These are *waymarks* and they do just that. The normal mark is a yellow arrow for a footpath, blue for a bridleway and red for a byway. Don't be surprised if the arrows on a path that you are following suddenly change colour. You have not necessarily gone wrong (though you may have!) — most probably the footpath has turned into a bridleway or byway, or vice versa.

Official long distance paths are marked by a white acorn, the symbol of the Countryside Commission. Some of these appear as metal plaques, others are painted. Some official paths are also signposted. Unofficial long distance paths may not be marked at all or may have a sign of local significance. The Cotswold Way, for example, is marked with white circles; the Shropshire Way by white birds.

Other authorities may use other symbols. In the Pembrokeshire National Park a sign showing a walker carrying a rucksack indicates that you are on a short circular walk of not more than two miles of easy walking. Signs showing two or three such walkers indicate longer, more demanding walks.

Waymarks and signposts are a great help when you are following a route, but don't be too dependent on them. Some, unfortunately, may become vandalised, struck by lightning or eaten by horses; others may get overgrown and easy to miss. You will need the appropriate maps and/or guide books to make certain of the route.

25

There are now a great many official, and unofficial, paths throughout Britain. Some, like the famous Pennine Way, are officially designated by the Countryside Commission. Some are the responsibility of local authorities. Others have no official standing at all but exist simply because someone has worked out a route along existing rights of way and written a guide book to it. Even the publisher has designed a hundred mile walk — along canal towpaths, just to be different!

Details of long distance routes can be obtained fron the Ramblers' Association and from the Long Distance Walkers Association. A visit to your bookshop should lead you to books on the better known paths and to any unofficial ones that exist in your neighbourhood.

STILES AND SIGNS

The Local Authority is usually the Highway Authority responsible for public footpaths. It gives permission for stiles and gates to be erected across public highways. If a landowner does not maintain stiles or gates for which he is responsible he can be charged the cost of the Highway Authority doing the job.

The Highway Authority is legally required to have signposts erected at points where a public footpath joins a metalled road, unless the Parish Council agrees that a sign is not necessary.

Stiles may be made of wood, metal or, sometimes, stone. Most have to be climbed over. High, ladder stiles, such as those encountered on parts of the Offa's Dyke Path may make your walk even more strenuous. Derbyshire stiles often consist of two stone posts that you have to squeeze through — not always easy for the overweight! Stiles in dry-stone walls usually consist of steps made from several larger stones set into the wall. They are often easy to miss.

The presence of a sign or a stile does not guarantee that the path will be navigable, or even that you will be able to find it! This is where a map becomes an essential part of your equipment. Stiles are sometimes made for people other than walkers, for example shooting parties, farmers, forestry workers, so don't assume that a stile necessarily indicates a right of way.

Remember that gates and stiles are not only built to let you pass but also to prevent the farmer's animals from straying. Always close gates after passing through. If you are in a party make sure the message gets passed back to the last person.

TRESPASS

You could become a trespasser by accident if you took the wrong path. However, despite those all too common 'Trespassers will be prosecuted' signs this is not strictly true. Trespassers can be asked to leave, and can be put off the land if they refuse. They can be sued for damage to property or for continuous annoyance but not for trespass.

If you strayed into a field when a farmer was hunting rabbits and you were accidentally shot you could sue the farmer — if you survived! If a gun toting landowner threatened you, he or she would be committing a criminal offence and could be prosecuted.

26

But it is far better to avoid any aggravation by making sure that you don't trespass. This is where good planning and a map are important. However, if you encountered a bull in a field through which your path passed you might find it preferable to trespass to avoid him.

OBSTRUCTIONS

All ramblers encounter trouble on footpaths at some time or another. Gates or stiles where there is a public right of way are sometimes blocked or ringed with barbed wire. Wire fences may be erected across footpaths. Thick undergrowth or rubbish may block them. You have the right to remove such obstructions, using wire cutters if necessary. All cases of this sort should be reported to the local authority as soon as possible. However, try not to leave things so that farm animals can stray.

If a right of way crosses a field of crops you can still walk across it even though plants will be trodden down. If the crop is impenetrable (e.g. oilseed rape) you can walk around the edge of the field.

Most farmers are reasonable people and accept ramblers as an inevitable part of the country scene. Some are very helpful and will readily cooperate with local authorities, rambling organisations, etc., in helping walkers to pass through their land safely and without difficulty. But if walkers leave gates open, drop litter (which can sometimes be lethal to animals), or cause damage it is not surprising that they will be unpopular with those who make their living from the land.

A very few farmers are deliberately obstructive. Some have been known to cover footpath signs with fertilizer bags rather than have ramblers walk through their farmyard. Fierce dogs have been chained at each side of a path. False notices have been erected. If you encounter obstructions or deliberately created difficulties remember that you have your rights and can call on the Highway Authority for help. The Ramblers' Association collects information about obstructed footpaths and will, where possible, take action to remedy problems. In 1987 the RA initiated the first successful prosecution of a farmer for footpath obstruction. If you send information to the RA give as much detail as you can, including grid references (see chapter 7 if you don't know about these).

ARE YOU DRAWN TO WATER?

Access to lakes, rivers and canals depends on who owns the land around the water and whether there are public footpaths along the banks. Your Ordnance Survey map will tell you if there are any rights of way. If you can ramble alongside the water don't assume that you can also plonk in a fishing line, boat, swim or paddle. The chances are that you can't.

Reservoirs, canals, stretches of rivers and surrounding land may belong to Water Authorities, British Waterways Board, industry or private owners. A notice of ownership might be displayed near water together with masses of bylaws and rules, but if no information is to hand it would be wise to check with the management before entering unknown territory. British Waterways Board nowadays normally allow walkers to have unrestricted access to canal towpaths.

A BIT OF BEACHCOMBING?

If you want to toddle along a beach, with a paddle or bathe thrown in, that is usually all right (though nude bathing might be frowned upon!). Most seaside beaches are owned by local authorities who have dedicated the area for public use.

There are, of course, some stretches of shore which are privately owned or owned by the Ministry of Defence where access may be limited or not permitted. But you would expect to find notices about this.

NATURE RESERVES

You can visit many national nature reserves, but if you are uncertain about access it would be worthwhile to telephone the nearest office of the Nature Conservancy Council for information and permission.

These reserves are set aside and maintained for conservation so there will be rules to safeguard plants, rocks and wildlife. You should not chip rocks or take any away for garden rockeries. Wild flowers should not be picked and are now protected by law — not only in nature reserves but also in the countryside generally.

COMMONS

Commons were originally open land where local people could graze cattle, dig peat, or collect wood for burning. Over the centuries rights concerning commons have become separated: there may be rights of grazing, rights of digging, and so on. Some rights still exist for farmers and local folk but do not extend to the public. You are not allowed to take your pet pony, rabbit or goat to a common where you personally have no rights and do not live.

The National Trust own some common land, as do other bodies, but this does not mean that the public have automatic access. Epping Forest, Bexhill Downs and the Clent Hills are three examples of common land which do have public access.

PLOUGHING UP FOOTPATHS

A farmer may not legally plough up a footpath or byway running along the headland of a field. (The headland is the border of a field where the plough turns and so has to be ploughed separately.) In fact this does sometimes happen and ramblers are forced to walk in a ditch or up against the hedge because a footpath has been ploughed out.

Where a footpath crosses arable land the farmer can plough it but must, by law, make good the surface, normally within six weeks. Quite often the surface is just left as it is and ramblers' feet make it walkable.

THE COUNTRYSIDE COMMISSION

The Countryside Commission came into being by virtue of the Countryside Act 1968 and does a grand job. The Commission own no land but are responsible for the conservation of natural beauty in England and Wales. They encourage the provision and improvement of facilities for the enjoyment of the countryside. They advise on policy, give technical help, do research and experimental work, and designate areas of outstanding landscape as national parks.

They are responsible for the major long distance paths. If you feel an urge to tackle these there are plenty to choose from — but make sure that you are fit enough to tackle the mileage before setting off.

SOME LONG DISTANCE PATHS.

This is a personal choice of some of the best known paths. It is not complete and many others exist. The distances given are the 'official' figures. In practice the actual distances may be somewhat greater.

Cleveland Way. 93 miles from Helmsley to Filey, across the North Yorkshire moors and then along the North-East Coast.

Coast to Coast Walk. 190 miles from St. Bees Head on the West Coast, through the Lake District, the Yorkshire Dales and the North Yorkshire Moors, to Robin Hood's Bay on the East Coast.

Cotswold Way. 100 miles through the Cotswold Hills from Chipping Campden to Bath.

Dales Way. 81 miles through the Yorkshire Dales from Ilkley in West Yorkshire to Bowness-on-Windermere in the Lake District.

North Downs Way. 140 miles through the Kent Downs and Surrey Hills from Farnham to Dover.

Offa's Dyke Path. 168 miles along the English/Welsh border from Chepstow in the south to Prestatyn on the North Wales coast. It takes its name from the eighth century earthwork built by Offa, King of Mercia.

Peddars Way. 86 miles from Knettishall near Thetford to Cromer. The only official long distance path in East Anglia.

Pembrokeshire Coast Path. 168 miles following the Pembrokeshire coastline from Amroth to St. Dogmaels near Cardigan.

Pennine Way. 250 miles from Edale in Derbyshire to Kirk Yetholm in the Scottish Borders. The first of Britain's long distance paths and the most popular.

Ridgeway Path. 85 miles through the North Wessex Downs and the Chilterns from Ivinghoe Beacon, near Tring to Overton Hill, near Avebury in Wiltshire.

Shropshire Way. A circular walk of 125 miles between Wem in the north and Ludlow in the south.

South Downs Way. 80 miles from Eastbourne following the South Downs ridge to Buriton. This way is also open to horseriders and cyclists.

South West Peninsula Coast Path (South West Way). 515 miles round the south west peninsula from Studland in the south to Minehead in the north. It is divided into four sections: Dorset, South Devon, Cornwall, and Somerset and North Devon.

Staffordshire Way. 93 miles from Mow Cop to Kinver Edge.

Thames Walk. 150 miles along the River Thames from Putney in London to Thames Head in Oxfordshire.

Viking Way. 140 miles from the Humber Bridge to Oakham in Leicestershire. It is linked to the Wolds Way by a walkway across the Humber Bridge.

West Highland Way. Scotland's first long distance path. 92 miles from Milngavie on the outskirts of Glasgow to Fort William.

Wolds Way. A continuation of the Cleveland Way, this path goes through 70 miles of the Yorkshire Wolds from Filey to North Ferriby on the Humber.

5

Preserving the Countryside

The British countryside is a precious inheritance which is under threat from many sources — industry, mining interests, industrialised farming, the building trade, the road lobby, etc. Ramblers, through organisations such as the National Trust, the Ramblers' Association, environmental groups, etc. can help to fight these threats. But walkers themselves can also present a threat if they behave in a careless or irresponsible manner. Although we go out to enjoy the countryside remember that it is also where other people live and work and on which they are deoendent for their living. So please remember the following:

FASTEN ALL GATES

This is most important to prevent farm animals from straying. Leaving gates open seems to be a sin that farmers (rightly) never forgive or forget. Animals that stray can cause havoc on farms and on public roads, and can do immense damage to crops.

In a group the first rambler, usually the leader, will open the gate and then see that it is closed after all have followed. If the party is a large one the leader should designate a member as 'back marker' responsible for seeing that all gates are closed. Otherwise, he should shout 'gate' and this message should be passed back to the rear. The last person through must then close the gate.

GUARD AGAINST FIRES

In any season it is possible for a fire to break out, particularly during a dry spell and regardless of temperature. Forest fires can start through lightning or can be ignited by careless smokers — the latter being probably the most common cause.

Fire in a high wind is very dangerous to all life and can spread at an alarming rate, doing immense damage on the way. If you spot a fire report it by telephone, as quickly as you can, to the nearest fire brigade, police station or Forestry Commission office. Don't hesitate to approach the nearest house or farm to ask to use their telephone.

"Gate!"

But make sure that it is a wild fire and not a farmer clearing gorse or burning off corn stubble. These fires can sometimes look alarming but are normally harmless — though, remember, they can occasionally get out of hand.

If you have secret dreams about living rough and free, cooking whatever is caught over an open fire, forget it and stick to the cheese sandwiches. In any case it is an offence (coming under the heading of criminal damage) to light a fire without the permission of the landowner.

KEEP TO PUBLIC PATHS

It's common sense to keep to footpaths across farmland and through woods — and, indeed, illegal to stray from them. The public do not have free access to land surrounding public highways — and to roam about anywhere could simply antagonise farmers and landowners.

Dry-stone walls, if climbed over, are all too easily damaged and a gap in them could allow sheep and cattle to stray. This does nothing to help the rambler image.

LEAVE WELL ALONE

All farm machinery should be left well alone. Children, for their own good, should not be allowed to meddle.

Don't handle livestock. It might be tempting to pick up new born lambs, or stroke calves, but farmers won't thank you for it.

Leave growing crops alone. Public footpaths sometimes go through fruit growing areas and orchards, but remember that all fruit, including windfalls, belongs to the farmer.

DON'T BE A LITTER LOUT

Litter is one of the curses of modern living. But who wants drink cans, crisp bags, paper, sweet wrappers and cigarette packets scattered all over a beautiful landscape? Thoughtful ramblers always take their rubbish away with them.

If you are walking in a National Park you may come across a volunteer warden picking up litter. If you carry a spare plastic bag you could always help!

KEEP WATER CLEAN

Water in the countryside is vital for plant, animal and human use. Never do anything to make it dirty or undrinkable.

DOGS

If taken on a walk dogs must always be under close control — and for most pets this means being constantly on a lead. Dogs unused to the countryside tend to go slightly mad, despite normally being well behaved. Man's best friend can spoil a ramble for both owner and other walkers when it won't obey commands, leave cattle or sheep alone, or come when called.

LOOK RIGHT — LOOK LEFT

Because country roads are quieter than busy city streets, walkers are sometimes tempted to amble about the tarmac from side to side without taking much care. But rural drivers can hurtle about just as fast as town motorists. It is wise to take normal precautions and always walk facing the oncoming traffic.

Sometimes a country road can be filled by cattle or sheep on the way to farm, field or market. If you meet a herd or flock keep into the side of the road and, to avoid confusing them, stand still until they have passed.

NOISE

Ramblers, thank goodness, don't walk about with stereo radios blasting the peace with heavy rock. The countryside is peaceful and in many places there are bylaws to keep it that way. It is, in fact, an offence to cause unnecessary noise or annoyance on a public highway.

THE COUNTRY CODE

This was devised by the Countryside Commission and summarises the dos and don'ts for walkers in the country.

Guard against all risk of fire.
Fasten all gates.
Keep dogs under proper control.
Keep to the paths across farm land.
Avoid damaging fences, hedges and walls.
Leave no litter — take it home.
Safeguard water supplies.
Protect wild life, wild plants and trees.
Go carefully on country roads.
Respect the life of the countryside.

METAL DETECTORS

If you are a treasure seeker with a metal detector forget it when you go rambling. You are not allowed to disturb the surface of the ground or to pocket any object that the detector might find. Digging holes on public access land can result in prosecution for trespass, criminal damage or theft. This also applies to beaches. Many local authorities display notices forbidding the use of metal detectors.

CARS

Should you drive out into the countryside to the start of a ramble be careful where you park your Porsche. You may not drive off the road or park without the permission of the landowner or occupier. If your motor is left on the road be sure that it does not cause an obstruction to other road users. To leave a car off the road on a verge, in a field or wood, or on a common, is an offence.

It is wise to sort out where you are going to park before you set out. There are public car parks at most popular places. The Forestry Commission, the National Trust and other bodies provide them as part of the walking scene. Remember that car parks are now shown on Ordnance Survey maps.

There is an increasing danger today of parked cars being broken into — even out in the country. Never leave things on seats where they are visible to thieves. Even items left in the boot of a car may not be safe. Anything that you do not want with you when walking is best left at home.

"Which one of you cut this down?"

6

How to get lost

If you want to get lost when you go out into the countryside the answer is simple. Just don't bother with a map or compass: simply trust your instinct for direction. If you are right-handed you will tend to walk in a clockwise direction; if a lefty in an anti-clockwise one. The size of the circle can vary between a few hundred yards and a few miles. The result should be fun!

But it is better to learn some simple navigational skills. Getting lost is not going to do much much for a family ramble. Children will become bored and tired, and storms may blow up on the matrimonial front. So, in this chapter, let us look at maps and then, in the next chapter, at using a compass.

DEFINITIVE MAPS

These are the principal sources of information about public footpaths, bridleways and byways. They are held by County and Borough Councils and are used by the Ordnance Survey in the compilation of some of their maps. The detail on definitive maps goes back in history to when the information was gathered from local people and from Parish Councils. However, not all of the country is covered by these maps.

If you are a local historian or a nut for maps you may be able to inspect definitive maps at council offices or local libraries. Many joyful hours lurking in dusty storerooms awaits you!

ORDNANCE SURVEY MAPS

These are the maps most used by walkers. They are crammed with useful information and cover the whole of Great Britain. They don't cost a fortune (unless you want to buy the complete set) and can be easily obtained from book shops, outdoor shops, Government (HMSO) bookshops or direct from the Ordnance Survey. The most useful is the Pathfinder series which is to a scale of 1:25,000 (4 centimetres to 1 kilometre, or 1 inch to 2½ miles). Also useful, though not carrying so much detail, is the Landranger series. This is to a scale of 1:50,000 (2 centimetres to 1 kilometre or 1 inch to 1¼ miles). Pathfinders each cover an area of 10km x 20km, Landrangers 40km x 40km.

Both the Pathfinder and the Landranger series show public footpaths and bridleways. The principal difference between the two is that Pathfinders also show field boundaries — a great help when you are in unknown country. Also, the larger scale does make for easier reading, especially if your eyes are no longer in the first flush of youth. A magnifying glass can come in very handy at times, and can be invaluable if you are caught without a torch and are stuggling to read a map when it is growing dusk.

You can also obtain very large scale maps (1:2,500 or 25 inches to the mile) from Government bookshops or the Ordnance Survey. They are very good for easy map reading and provide very detailed information. On them, buildings, roads, railways, almost all permanent tracks, fences, hedges, ponds, rivers and many other features are shown. The disadvantage for walkers is that many more than one would be needed on a normal day's ramble. Each map covers only an area of 2km by 1km (200 hectares, 494.2 acres).

The Landranger series covers Great Britain with 204 maps, starting in the Shetlands Islands with No. 1 and finishing in Cornwall with No. 204.

In the Pathfinder series there will be a total of 1373 maps when they have all been issued. The Pathfinders are replacing the old 2½ inch series and in some parts of the country the latter may be the only ones currently available. Although they are the same scale each map covers only half the area of the Pathfinders.

Outdoor Leisure Maps, also produced by the Ordnance Survey, are to a scale of 1:25,000 but include a larger area than the Pathfinder series. They cover the more popular recreational areas including the Lake District, the Peak District, the Brecon Beacons, Snowdonia, the North Yorkshire Moors, Dartmoor and several others.

All maps give the date when they were last revised. It is important to know this because things can sometimes change quickly. Old woods can vanish, new woods can be planted, housing estates can appear, railway lines can be closed, old buildings can be demolished, man-made lakes can appear and rivers change course. The old map given you by your dad may be of no use when you are planning a ramble.

The date on a map is also useful for calculating what is known as the Magnetic Variation which is needed for very accurate route planning. Many folk stroll through life thinking that there is only one 'North' but there are three:

1. True North. This is the direction of the North Pole.
2. Grid North. This is shown on Ordnance Survey maps by vertical lines from bottom to top, so you take the top of the map as being North. Grid North is not quite the same thing as True North because the earth is a sphere whereas maps are flat. If you don't understand that go and talk to a mathematician — but it makes no difference for rambling (unless you want to walk to the North Pole).
3. Magnetic North. This is the spot that compass needles point to. It varies slowly over the years and the difference between its present value and Grid North is known as the Magnetic Variation — more about this in the next chapter. According to scientists Magnetic North and South change places every few million years or so — but that's unlikely to bother us.

SIGNS AND SYMBOLS

Ordnance Survey maps carry a list of the conventional signs used on them. Many are self explanatory but it is well worth while spending some time studying the list and getting familiar with the less obvious ones. They are all very useful to walkers. We can tell at a glance what kind of wood is being approached, firs (conifers), broad-leaved (deciduous — trees which shed their leaves in winter) or mixed. Ramblers generally love broad-leaved woods with their variety of wildlife. They dislike coniferous areas, many planted by the Forestry Commission, which they find dark, gloomy, regimented and lacking in character and wildlife. Some, however, are managed imaginatively and can be quite pleasant.

We can look for landmarks such as churches which may have spires or towers or neither. A railway can be seen running along an embankment, then vanishing into a cutting. We are warned about Ministry of Defence ranges, open pits, refuse tips and quarries. We can home in on youth hostels, public houses, post offices, car parks, picnic sites, Roman villas, and many other useful and interesting features.

41

Especially valuable, of course, are footpaths, bridle paths and byways. Those shown in red on the 1:50,000 maps and green on the 1:25,000 maps indicate rights of way. You have a legal right to walk along these and the landowner has a legal responsibilty to ensure that they are not blocked or ploughed out — a responsibilty which, unfortunately, is too often ignored. Footpaths marked in black are not legal rights of way but some, nevertheless, may be well used because the owner permits their use (concessionary paths). Unfortunately some footpaths (even if legal rights of way) are difficult to find on the ground because of the presence of crops or simply because they have not been walked regularly in recent years. Concessionary paths through grouse moors may be closed on certain days when shooting is taking place.

"Maybe the blue lines are rivers?"

CONTOUR LINES

If you are new to maps you may, at first, find these lines somewhat confusing. They are printed in orange and show positions of equal height (in metres) above mean sea level. They are spaced at intervals of 10 metres with the height marked on them.

Contour lines provide a picture of the shape of the land. When lines are close together we are on a steep hill or mountain. Spaced out contours indicate a gradual climb or descent. The way contours bend in and out indicates a valley or spur. A stream or river (marked in blue) running down a valley can be clearly picked out. The highest point of a hill is indicated by a number (in black figures) giving its height in metres above mean sea level— this is known as a 'spot height'.

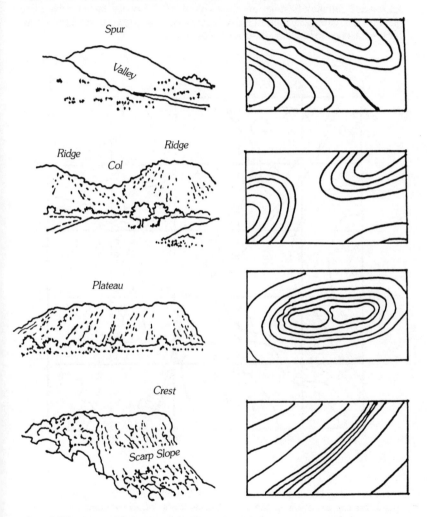

Some hill features and their map contours.

Contours are a great aid to our knowing where we are and what lies ahead or about us.

MAP REFERENCES

Ordnance Survey maps are divided into squares of equal size. These are numbered along the top, bottom and sides of the map and are needed to pin-point exact locations. The figures along the top and bottom are known as Eastings (because they are measured in an easterly direction) and those along the sides are known as Northings. Eastings are always given first — you will be in trouble if you get them the wrong way round! Grid references are usually given to six figures, three for the Eastings followed by three for the Northings.

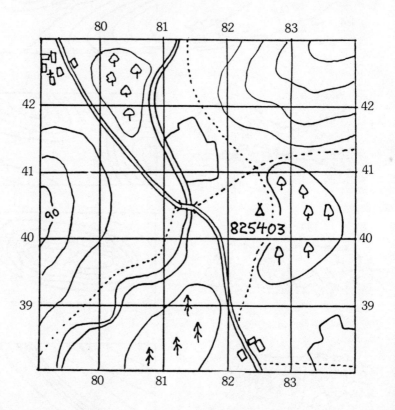

For the camp site reference shown in the illustration first read the number of the line at the top or bottom of the map which is to the left of the camp site — in this case it is 82. Now mentally subdivide the distance between 82 and 83 into ten equal parts and decide on which of these the camp site is to be found. In our case it is about half way between 82 and 83, or five subdivisions. So the Easting is 825. Now do the same with the side scale. This, as you can see, is 40 plus about a third — three subdivisions, say. This gives 403. The complete reference then is 825403.

"Frank! The map, the map!"

There are various mnemonics for remembering which comes first, Eastings or Northings. Try "along the top and down the sides", or work out your own. You might like to devise map reading games with a walking companion. Take turns in giving and finding objects by grid references. The loser could do the washing up for a week.

To make a grid reference unique it needs to be preceded by two letters. The Ordnance Survey divide the whole of Great Britain into 100 km squares and each of these is given a two letter reference which is shown in large blue letters on Landranger maps. Your complete reference might then be SP825403. However, since you will usually know where you want to be within a 100 km range you won't usually need to bother with the letters.

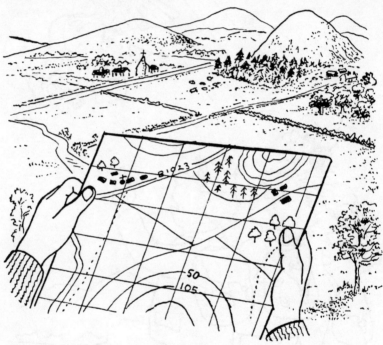

Setting your map with what you see.

GETTING STARTED

First obtain a map of the district in which you live, or one that you know well. A country district is preferable. Urban areas, where streets dominate the map, are generally less interesting and, in any case, really need a larger scale than the Landranger or Pathfinder series. Then walk around part of the area and pick out features on the ground and relate them to the corresponding features on the map. As well as providing some happy hours walking you will rapidly become familiar with the signs and symbols. If you can sit in a high place where you have a good view over a wide area, spread the map out in front of you and see how it relates to your view.

As you walk around you can use a map in two ways. You can treat it like a book, always keeping it the same way up, with North at the top. That makes it easier to read the place names and some of the symbols, but to many this is the harder way and the one likely to give a beginner most problems.

The other way is to set the map in line with the ground in front of you. This means that you turn the map to align with what you see, and as you walk you move the map to correspond with what you come to. If you start correctly like this and are careful you will always know where you are at any time. The first method needs a lot of mental juggling because you have to remember that the map is only pointing in one direction when, in fact, this might mean that it is upside down, or sideways, to your direction of travel. If you have a good head for remembering that left is really right and that up is down this system is ideal and it enables you to leave the map hanging round your neck in a map case. But otherwise use the second, more widely used way.

KNOW THE JARGON

It is helpful if you understand the terms used by experienced walkers. Here are some of the more common ones.

BECK or BURN: a mountain stream.
COL: a depression in a line of hills or along a ridge. A col is also known as a saddle. It sometimes provides an easy route (a pass) through high ground.
ESCARPMENT or SCARP: a ridge with a steep, cliff-like, slope on one side and a more gentle slope on the other. The highest point is the CREST.
FELL: a mountain in the Lake District or the Pennines. Sometimes used as a term for moorland.
KNOLL: a small, rounded hill.
MOOR: high ground, usually covered in heather.
MOUNTAIN: a high mass of land over 2000 ft (600 m) high. Below this it is a HILL.
PLATEAU: a flat (table top) area on high ground.
RIDGE: a long stretch of fairly level high ground with the ground falling away sharply on each side.
SCREE: an area of loose broken rock on the side of a mountain.
SPUR: high ground which projects out into lower ground.
SUMMIT: the highest point of a hill or mountain.
TARN: a mountain lake.
VALLEY: a depression, which may be long or short, between higher ground. Valleys often have streams or rivers running down them. Others may be dry.

As an exercise try to pick out these features on a map. Use one covering a mountainous area, for example the Lake District.

When you are planning a walk it is very useful to be able to build up in your mind a picture of the sort of terrain you will be walking through. Practice with this skill will greatly help you in planning walks and plotting routes accurately.

TRIG POINTS

A trig point (triangulation point) is marked on the map by a triangle with a dot in the centre. The height above sea level is given alongside.

On the ground there is a concrete triangular pillar with metal insets on the top for supporting surveying instruments used by the Ordnance Survey in map making. Trig points are a favourite background for ramblers to pose against when being photographed. Trig points are all numbered — a few ramblers collect these numbers in the way train spotters collect engine numbers.

NOTE

In recent years the Ordnance Survey have made several changes to their maps. They are now all in metric format ____ previoulsy those corresponding to today's Landranger and Pathfinder series were the 1 inch to the mile series and the 2½ inches to the mile series. After metrication the first new maps still carried the old contour lines, at 50 yd intervals but given in metres — rather confusing! The latest maps have been revised and the contour lines are at 10 metre intervals.

Woodland, on the old maps, was always indicated as coniferous, broad-leaved or mixed. After metrication the Ordnance Survey dropped this differentiation and showed all woodlands by a uniformly green area. That led to a lot of complaints from ramblers and others and maps have now reverted to the original system.

7

Which Way?

Before you can make effective use of a map in an unknown locality you need to know where North is. Birds, seemingly, know this by instinct but we humans have to rely on the compass. This is an essential item of equipment for ramblers. The simplest compass will point North as accurately as the most expensive. However a good instrument will have a number of additional features that will be of considerable assistance when you are navigating — especially if weather conditions or the terrain are difficult.

A compass can be used for picking the right path through wide open spaces such as moors or huge corn fields, for keeping to a safe path when you are in thick fog, for finding exactly where you are, or for locating distant features — such as the nearest pub or Mountain Rescue Post — provided that you know how to use it correctly.

The only cause of a compass malfunction is the presence of magnetic material, usually iron or steel. So when you are using it keep your compass well away from any metal objects. A watch strap, camera, belt buckle or metal buttons might cause you to go miles off course. In some locations 'magnetic anomalies' are caused by the presence of magnetic ores in nearby rocks and they can affect your compass needle. There is nothing you can do about these other than regularly checking your position against the map. But they might provide an excuse if you get your walking party lost! A magnetic storm can have a similar effect.

The best compass for walkers is the Silva or similar model. These are not too expensive and can be purchased from most sports and outdoor shops.

Start by spending some time studying the design of your compass and carefully reading the instructions that come with it. If it is a Silva or similar model (p.50) be sure that you can recognise the orienting lines (A), the orienting arrow (B), the direction arrow (C) and which is the North pointing end of the magnetic needle (D). Note that the compass housing swivels on the rectangular base: this is a most valuable feature in direction finding.

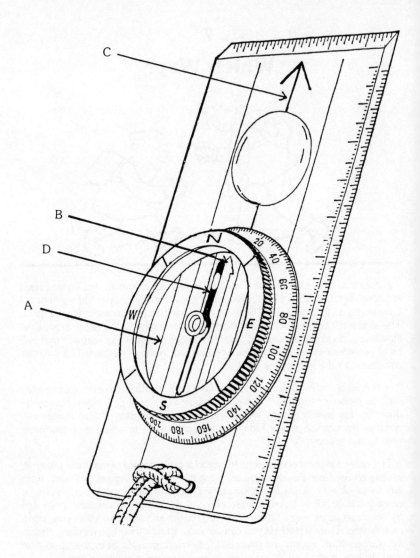

COMPASS BEARINGS

The compass housing, as well as being marked with the four points of the compass (N, S, E, W), is also marked out with a scale of degrees. A compass bearing is a direction given by this scale. A bearing of 45 degrees will take you in a north-easterly direction, a 315 degrees bearing will take you north-west. The bearing shown in the diagram is 200 degrees and is roughly south south-west. As you will see, bearings are measured clockwise from north.

50

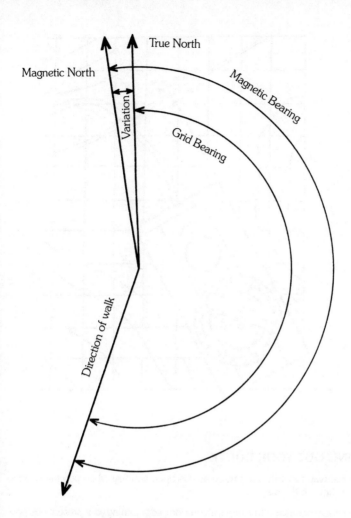

MAGNETIC VARIATION

Because the magnetic north is in Northern Canada and moves gradually over the years it is necessary, for accurate compass work, to make small adjustments when transferring compass bearings to grid bearings on the map, and vice versa.

Your Ordnance Survey map gives the appropriate magnetic variation and the date of that value. The value of the annual variation is also given. On the Landranger series this appears at the top of the map together with an arrow showing the actual direction of magnetic north at the time the map was produced. On other maps it appears with the list of symbols.

For example, the magnetic variation was 6 deg W of Grid North in June 1985 and was varying annually by about 9 mins E.

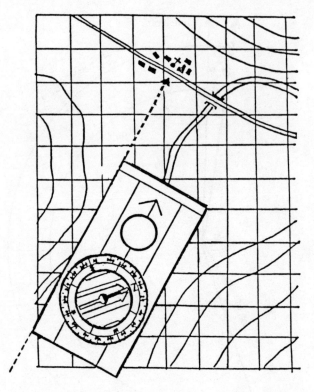

fig. 1

WORKING OUT YOUR ROUTE

This is the way to work out a route across open country when you know your present position on the map.

1. Place the compass on the map with one long edge joining your present position to the point that you want to reach and with the direction arrow pointing towards your destination (fig. 1).
2. Turn the compass housing until the orienting lines on it are parallel with the grid lines of the map and the orienting arrow points to the top of the map (fig. 2).
3. Still holding the compass firmly against the map rotate the compass housing anti-clockwise by the angle of the Grid Magnetic Variation. The orienting arrow will now be pointing on the map to Magnetic North. (You can omit this step if your destination is not far away. However, if the Magnetic Variation is 6 degrees, say, you will be a tenth of a mile off course after you have walked a mile.)
4. Take the compass off the map and turn it horizontally until the red (North) end of the needle is parallel with the orienting lines. Now the direction arrow is pointing to your destination (fig. 3). If you want to know your bearing you can read this, in degrees, from the scale.

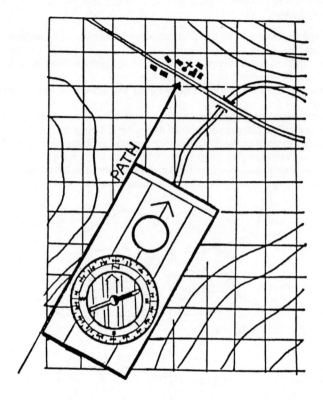

fig. 2

If you are travelling any distance you need to make a periodic check of your direction. The best way to do this is to proceed in a series of steps. Identify some prominent feature in front of you on your required route and walk towards it. When you reach it pick out another feature ahead and walk towards that.

Of course in mist that method may not be possible. Then you could direct one member of the walking party forward by a reasonable distance to act as a marker, waiting for the party to catch up and then repeating the procedure until you reach your destination. It will slow you down but better that than getting lost. Buy the marker a pint when you reach the next pub.

FINDING WHERE YOU ARE

If you know where you are on the map and want to identify a village or some feature in the distance:

1. Hold the compass so that the direction arrow is pointing to the feature you want to identify.
2. Rotate the compass housing so that the orienting arrow is lined up with the compass needle and pointing Magnetic North.
3. Rotate the compass housing clockwise by the amount of the Magnetic Variation.
4. Place the compass on the map near to your present position and so that the orienting lines of the compass are parallel with the grid lines of the map. Slide the compass across the map, keeping these lines parallel, until one long edge of the compass touches your present position. If the feature you want to identify is reasonably close it will now also be somewhere along the long edge of the compass. If it is further away it will be somewhere along the line of the long edge (fig. 4).

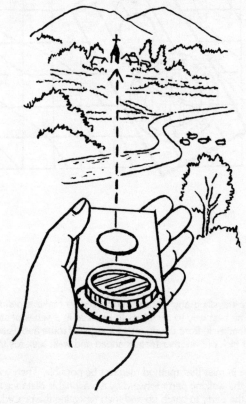

fig. 3

54

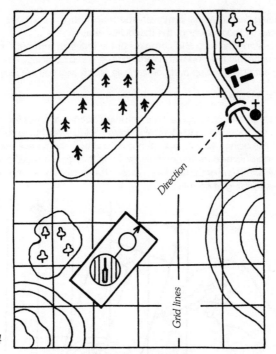

fig. 4

Suppose, however, that you only have an approximate idea of where you are and you want to find your actual position. You now need to take two bearings (cross bearings) and use the procedure known as resection.

Look around you for some prominent features that you can also identify on the map — a church with a spire, a small lake, a radio mast, anything that you can take a bearing on.

Choose one of these features and proceed as described (1 - 4) above. Then, when you have lined up the compass on the map draw a pencil line on the map along the long edge of the compass (fig. 5). Now take another feature and repeat the procedure (fig. 6). You now have two lines — where they cross is your present position on the map. If necessary extend the lines until they meet.

MAP SETTING

In the previous chapter I suggested that you would probably prefer to use a map by setting it in line with the ground around you. If for some reason you can't do that (perhaps because you are walking over rather featureless moorland) you can use your compass to set it.

1. Hold the map flat and put the compass on it in your approximate position. Turn the compass until the compass orienting lines are parallel with the grid lines on the map.

2. Holding the compass firmly on the map turn the compass housing anti-clockwise by the amount of the magnetic variation.

3. Still holding the map and compass firmly together, turn both round until the compass needle lines up with North on the compass scale. The map and the ground are now lined up and you can see which way you are facing.

BACK BEARING

Suppose that after setting out on a compass bearing a dense fog descends and you cannot see more than a few feet. You decide not to go on but to go home, despite the lawn grass being two feet high. What do you do? You retrace your steps using a back bearing. Turn yourself round and walk on the opposite needle setting — that is, using the South end of the needle in place of the North. There is no need to disturb the compass setting to do this.

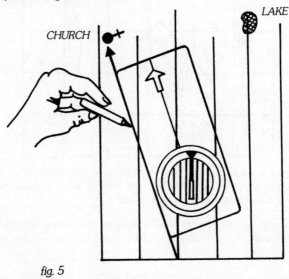

fig. 5

COME BACK, ALL IS FORGIVEN

To test your skill with a compass try walking in a triangle and returning to the exact spot you started from. Amaze your spouse, children, friends, dog, with this trick.

Put a mark of some sort on the ground, then walk off with the direction arrow set at 120 degrees on your compass. Remember that as you follow the direction arrow you must keep the compass needle pointing to North on the dial. Count fifty paces as you go, stop and add 120 to your compass bearing, making it now 240 degrees. Walk another fifty paces on this, pause, add another 120 degrees and walk straight forward another fifty paces to return to your mark. If you end up somewhere else go back to the start of this chapter.

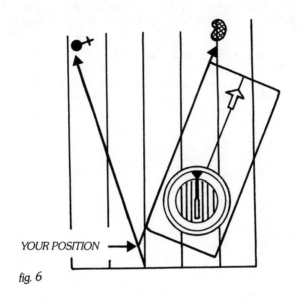

YOUR POSITION →

fig. 6

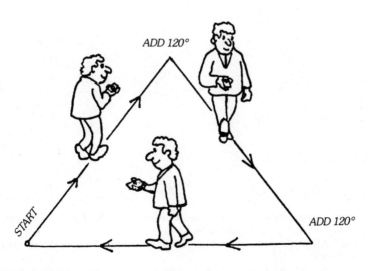

ADD 120°

ADD 120°

START

A compass walk

57

You can take this method further by using it out on a moor and walking a larger triangle. Be sure to measure your distances accurately either by a reliable pedometer or by careful timing and an even pace. Have a good marker — a pile of rocks, a heap of vegetation or whatever is at hand. You might be able to scratch your name in sandy soil.

AVOIDING OBSTACLES BY COMPASS

If you are out walking on a compass bearing and come to an obstacle, a deep swamp for instance, you will have to make a detour. By following this simple method you can get back to your original route.

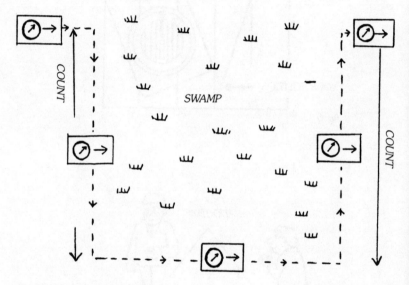

Avoiding an obstacle with compass.

1. Change direction by exactly 90 degrees. Walk clear of the obstacle, remembering to count your paces.
2. Change direction by another 90 degrees and walk forward until past the obstacle.
3. Make another 90 degree turn and walk the same number of paces as in step 1.
4. Turn another 90 degrees and you can now continue forward on your original route.

WATCH IT

If, through forgetfulness or other misfortune, you don't have your compass, you can use your watch, provided the sun is shining, to find the direction of South. Hold the watch flat so that the hour hand points to the sun. A matchstick or pencil held

upright over the end of the hour hand will cast a shadow over the face and give the correct position. Then bisect (halve) the angle between the hour hand and 12 (for Greenwich Mean Time), 1 (for British Summer Time) or 2 (for Double British Summer Time) — this line then points South.

If you have a digital watch just draw a watch face on a piece of paper and use that.

PRACTICE MAKES PERFECT

Good compass work requires a fair degree of experience. Practice all the methods described in this chapter in some part of the country that you know reasonably well. When you walk with a club try to follow the route on your own map. Many leaders are happy to help walkers who are eager to learn.

Many rambling clubs run short courses from time to time on map reading and compass work. If your club holds one try to go on it.

"Go on — it's a right of way."

8

Hazards

Walking in the countryside — or even out on wild moors or mountains — is a lot safer than many common activities like crossing the road or travelling in a car. And remember that the majority of accidents take place in the home. But, nevertheless, there are some hazards in the great outdoors and it is as well to be prepared so that if you encounter them you will know what to do.

BULLS

The present law allows farmers to keep a bull on land which is crossed by a public footpath provided that the bull is not more than ten months old or that it is kept with cows and is not one of the breeds considered to be dangerous, especially the dairy breeds such as Friesians, Jerseys and Guernseys. Many ramblers are city folk who can't be expected to know the difference between a French Charolais and a British Friesian so it is wise to treat all bulls with suspicion. But don't panic!

Always watch a bull, never walk between it and cows, keep quiet and don't run. Contrary to popular belief bulls are not attracted to red clothes although they are attracted to movement. They may see sudden activity as a threat. If you can, keep near to a hedge or fence that you can get through if a bull starts to appear aggressive.

Give a wide berth to any bull that seems aggressive. Report the location and all details to the Highway Authority for the area.

If you do find yourself facing a bull, look for danger signals. An aggressive bull will snort, bellow, paw the ground, lower its head and flatten back its ears before it charges.

If, in spite of your keeping still, the bull seems likely to charge, the only thing to do is to get out of its way quickly by sprinting to the nearest safe place. Throw off a jacket or other piece of clothing — the bull may decide to attack this before you. Bulls are rather clumsy so, if you keep calm, you should be able to dodge.

BULLOCKS AND HEIFERS

Some walkers are nervous of bullocks and heifers which are normally found in herds and are always very inquisitive. A group of ramblers will attract their attention and cause the whole herd to gallop over to watch. There is no need to be alarmed, but if they do get too close they can easily be sent off by just flapping your arms up and down. They retreat if they feel you are a bit dotty.

COWS

Cows are peaceful creatures but never go near one with a young calf and especially never between one and her youngsters. She may think you are up to no good and defend her family.

DOGS

When walking through or near a farm you may be confronted by what appears to be a fierce dog. Try not to show fear as this emotion seems to transmit to animals. Most barking dogs are simply giving a warning that you are on their territory and won't do anything more. Keep calm and talk to the dog in a friendly way. If it continues towards you stay still and keep talking gently to it. Let it sniff you if it wants to. Most times this will satisfy the dog and you can slowly back away.

To turn and run is to ask for trouble. This just excites aggressive animals.

If, in spite of your peaceful overtures, you are attacked, try to get hold of the animal by the ruff of its neck and gently move it somewhere safe — over a wall, into a barn or shed where you can close the door, anywhere it can't get at you. Don't grab its tail — it will almost certainly twist round and bite you.

ELECTRIC FENCES

Electric cattle fences are frequently encountered on walks in farming areas. They give a series of shocks which although unpleasant are not fatal — even if the farmer might not welcome your presence he will have no wish to electrocute his sheep or cattle!

You can test to see if an electric fence is on by lightly touching it with the back of your hand. To cross a live fence you can crawl underneath or else drape a coat or waterproof across it and then stride over. If an electric fence crosses a right of way a sensible farmer will have provided easy passage by running the wire through a piece of rubber hose.

THUNDERSTORMS

If you are caught out in the middle of the countryside by a sudden thunderstorm try to seek shelter fast. If you are forced to shelter in a wood, avoid the large trees and sit or lie some distance away from tree-trunks. Don't shelter under a solitary tree.

If you are out in the open where there is no shelter, on a moor or heath for example, lie down and cover up with anything waterproof. The idea, when there is lightning about, is to prevent yourself from being a projection above your surroundings — in other words, a lightning conductor.

If you are on a mountain top or ridge when you see lightning approaching get down to a lower level quickly. Lightning will hit and travel along a ridge, or hit a peak and move elsewhere. To get down fast, stay upright and zig zag down as rapidly as is consistent with safety. To sit down and slide is to lose control and possibly collect many abrasions and bruises.

In a storm stay calm, act quickly and you will be fine. Remember that it is better to be soaked than toasted.

"Coffee break or last rites?"

"I do think that's a patch of bog-asphodel!"

FOGS AND MISTS

Mist can come down suddenly on hills, moor or heath and catch out the unwary. So be prepared. The temperature will drop and you may need to don extra clothes and possibly waterproofs.

If you are in a group keep close together and make sure that no-one gets separated — this can be all too easy if the group is spread out. Even if visibility is down to a few feet you can still carry on with accurate compass bearings, or even retrace your steps on a reverse compass bearing (Chapter 7). However, if you have not been using a compass or if the terrain is very hazardous — swamp, mountain, cliff, etc. — you might best stay where you are and wait for conditions to improve. Many bad accidents have been avoided by doing this. At such times you will appreciate the logic of always carrying extra warm clothing.

If you are going into the mountains or other lonely or hazardous areas always tell someone what your intended route is and when you expect to return. Even if weather conditions seem ideal when you set out they can always change suddenly. And there is always the possibility of a twisted ankle or other accident, a lost or broken compass, a lost map.

SNOW STORMS

Walking in the snow can be a delightful experience but snow can present a hazard and needs to be treated with respect. Make sure that you are warmly dressed and that your toes and fingers are protected against frostbite. Walking for any distance in deep snow can be an exhausting experience so if conditions are difficult give careful thought to turning back.

A very heavy snowfall can result in everything previously visible vanishing under a white blanket. Even in the UK it is possible to become snow blind. A white-out, as it is called, can be very frightening.

Keep with your party and don't stare at the snow. It helps if you keep a hood well over your head and upper face. As in a mist you must trust your compass and know your way back.

Mountain walking in ice or snow requires special techniques and training by an expert. Keep well away if you don't have the necessary skills.

THE CHILL FACTOR

In severe cold a factor to be borne in mind is what is known as the chill factor of the wind. In cold conditions wind itself can be a major hazard: in a 25 mph wind a temperature of 20 deg F (-7 deg C) is eqivalent in its chilling effect to -15 deg F (-26 deg C). In a 35 mph wind it is equivalent to -20 deg F (-29 deg C). A properly clothed person should be in little danger in effective temperatures down to -20 deg F, but below this there is increasing danger from frostbite and hypothermia.

SWAMPS AND BOGS

Most areas of moorland contain boggy areas. Most are more a nuisance than a danger, but some are hazardous and there is the very occasional fatality. Look out for bright green patches of a moss-like plant which seems to grow on the surface of very deep mud. This acts as a natural warning to us. The presence of tufts of grass or heather usually indicates reasonably firm areas of ground.

A walking stick is useful for feeling out the depth of mud before treading in it. If you do find yourself sinking in a bog don't panic or thrash about. Call for help, fall as gently as possible onto your back, then spread out your arms and gently edge yourself towards firm ground.

CLIFFS

Coastal walks are usually a delight but cliff tops can be dangerous. Footpaths can erode into the sea and there can be rockfalls and landslips. Watch out for warning notices, heed them and never walk right at the edge of a cliff.

Be especially careful in high winds. If the wind is blowing towards the sea it is wise to strike inland and use another route. Even if the wind is blowing from the sea be on your guard for sudden gusts and changes of wind direction. Be especially careful when your path changes direction.

SEASHORE

When you are rambling along a seashore it is easy to forget that tides can come in fast. You can easily miss the sight of oncoming waves as you explore rock pools or search for pieces of eight and if your exit is prevented by cliffs it is all too easy to get cut off. Don't put yourself in a position where you can't get to safety easily.

9

When the going gets tough

Unless you are a glutton for the tough stuff most of your walks will probably be pretty moderate going. But now and again you will come to terrain that presents some difficulties. It helps to be aware of the likely problems in advance.

When faced with tough going you can be sure that the terrain will slow you down, so deliberately lose pace rather than struggle to keep your normal speed. It is a British trait to grumble when the going is hard, but it's also a national characteristic to see the funny side of things. It helps enormously to tackle the worst conditions cheerfully.

If you become breathless it is a sign that you are going too fast, so slow down. If you go at the right pace you should be able to tackle the steepest climb without having to pause to get your breath back.

GROWING CROPS

In theory these ought not to present a problem because footpaths through them should be clear. In reality there are many fields where footpaths have been ploughed out and not restored as the law requires. Some farmers who have indulged in this undesirable practice have been successfully prosecuted — but that is of little consolation when you find your way obstructed.

If the crops are not too high you can probably pick your way through them, keeping as closely as possible to the line of the right of way — your map reading skills may be needed here. Sometimes the tracks made by the wheels of a tractor will make the going easier. If you are in a party remember to cross in single file. Even if there is a good footpath it will normally only be wide enough for one person. If the crop is impenetrable probably the only solution is to go round the edge of the field. This might be difficult but is seldom impossible.

The hardest growing crop to cross is oilseed rape. This plant provides the bright yellow patches that we see in the countryside in the summer. It grows tall, tough and dense and can cover you with yellow stain. If you have a machete and some hours to spare you might be able to cut your way through. Better to make your way round the edge.

You should, of course, never walk through crops where there is no right of way.

PLOUGHED FIELDS

In winter, spring and late summer walkers frequently have to cross ploughed fields. Some of these, due to modern farming methods, can be vast.

"It's your turn to clean our boots."

Light soil will tread down fairly easily, but walking over soil containing a high proportion of clay will be hard and slow. Clay clings to the soles of boots and builds up, making each step a weight lifting exercise for the feet. A big field can be as tiring to walk across as a long hill climb.

Take this sort of terrain slowly and pause occasionally to knock off the accumulated mud. As for growing crops, always go across ploughed fields in single file.

ROCK

The need for stout footwear is brought home to you when crossing rock. This can be hard on feet, ankles and legs, not to mention stamina. Rock can be lethal when it is covered with ice.

Take rock slowly and watch every footstep. A walking stick, used as an aid to balance, is very useful.

When climbing up steep rocky inclines be careful not to dislodge rocks or boulders. These will fall with increasing speed and would be a dangerous threat to any walkers below.

If you dislodge a boulder shout 'below!'. This is the accepted warning call — not 'get out of it!' or 'duck!'.

"Below!"

SCREE

Scree consists of loose stones and small boulders on steep mountain slopes. It can be very tough on your boots. Going up scree is hard work, and coming down requires special techniques. Always take your time going up otherwise you could slip back after each step forward.

Some mountain walkers descend scree by running or trotting, digging in their heels on each step. It is like staying upright on a moving carpet of stones and, so it is said, looks much harder and frightening than it actually is. One of the most exciting scree slopes to come down is the Great Boulder Chute on Alisdair on Skye. This can take over an hour to climb but can be run down in less than a minute. The record is said to be eleven seconds! Scree running is perhaps one of the best ways of losing members of your party. It is dangerous and is not recommended!

If you prefer to avoid the athletics a walking stick for support is a great help. Always keep your feet flat to maximise contact with the ground.

PEAT

Peat is formed from decomposing vegetation and, when dry, is delightful to walk on because of its springy nature. At times it can become so wet as to be like a bog. Then it can be difficult and it's possible to sink up to your knees in the stuff. Under these conditions it is better, and less tiring, if you can walk around it. When you do walk across wet peat take your time and so conserve your energy.

MOORLAND

Heather, bracken, gorse and long grass can all be tiring to walk through. When wet this vegetation will catch out poor waterproofing of boots and clothes. Boots made of plastic or rubber are ideal for this kind of terrain although they lack the support given by leather boots.

CANAL TOWPATHS

Towpaths can provide excellent opportunities for all year round walking. It is usually necessary to travel single file because towpaths today are seldom as wide as they were when the canals were important commercial routes — and nobody wants an unexpected swim. Single file walking will cause a long party to get very strung out so it is important that the leader should not get too far ahead.

The terrain along canals can vary greatly: there can be stretches of mud, water, slippery banks, rocks, overhanging brambles, branches and trees, but, like most rambles, the tough bits are relatively few. A pair of secateurs can often come in useful.

Sometimes, however, you will come to a stretch of canal where the towpath has collapsed or has been completely grown over with impenetrable bushes and brambles. If you are planning a walk along a canal that is not known to you always bear this possibilty in mind. Have a map and compass so that you can work out a detour if the towpath becomes impossible.

Towpaths are often rich in wildlife. It is possible to see heron, kingfishers, dragon flies, wagtails, jumping fish (and anglers), and many wild flowers. If there is a fishing contest in progress take care not to stumble over fishing tackle or its owners.

I said "Don't get in front of the leader!"

SAND

Firm, damp sand is easy to walk across, but when it's dry it becomes difficult. Your feet will sink in and you will waste a lot of energy if you try to go at your normal pace. The art of walking along the seashore is to find the stretches of sand that are just moist enough to provide a firm surface, and to avoid the areas that are too dry or too wet.

SNOW AND ICE

Walking in the winter when there is fresh snow on the ground can be a delightful experience, but it does require extra care, especially if you are on high ground. Snow not only makes everything look different, it hides paths and features that you might be relying on for finding your route. You may have to be more reliant on the compass.

If the snow is more than a few inches deep, ploughing through it can be hard work and will slow you down considerably. Watch out for drifts where you might find yourself up to your middle.

Frozen snow can be easier to walk on, though if it is deep, and frozen only on the surface, you may sometimes find yourself breaking through and having to scramble out of a drift.

If there is only a thin layer of snow be on your guard against the possibility of ice underneath it — these are the conditions when you are most likely to come a cropper!

MOUNTAINS

Mountain walking is a subject that fills numerous books and there are many pleasures in heading off to the hills on a fine day. If you are new to walking it would be wise, at first, to go out with someone who has experience. Remember to keep to a modest pace when you are climbing: if you get out of breath you are going too fast. Always take care, look where you are putting your feet, and keep an eye on changing weather conditions (see chapter 16).

Keep your feet flat — avoid the tendency that some walkers have to throw their weight onto their toes. On a steep climb or descent it helps to traverse — that is to make a series of zig-zags. This increases the distance but decreases the steepness of climb or descent.

Descending is often more difficult than climbing because it puts much more strain on leg and ankle muscles. Be especially careful on wet rock.

Traversing up and down steep hills.

Good footwear is particularly important when you are walking in the mountains. Rock and scree will soon rip through inadequate boots.

Don't forget to put the extra pullover in your rucksack: temperatures drop by about 3 degrees Fahrenheit for every 1000 ft of ascent (0.6 degrees Celsius per 100 m).

IN EMERGENCY...

When you are walking in the mountains or, indeed, anywhere that is lonely or hazardous you should have at least one whistle per group or family. It can be used to give the international distress signal if conditions become desperate or if there is an accident. The signal is six long blasts repeated at minute intervals until help comes.

You should also carry a torch and this can be used, at night, to flash the same signal. An alternative is to flash the Morse code SOS sign. This is three quick flashes, followed by three long flashes, then three quick ones again (. . . __ __ __ . . .).

The voice can be magnified in the mountains so you can also shout to try to summon aid. However, for this reason you should not shout other than for help. There are many false alarms each year, some of which endanger would-be rescuers.

Always display as much colour as possible — any members with bright cagoules or anoraks should display or wave them if mountain rescue teams and/or helicopters are alerted to look for you. It is surprising how insignificant you are in the mountains.

10
Looking after yourself

When you become hooked on rambling you will probably try longer and tougher walks, and then even the most careful of walkers can have minor accidents or misfortunes. If you learn how to deal with these before they happen you will be less likely to need the help of others, and also, if necessary, be able to come to the assistance of someone in trouble.

Some training in first aid is, of course, always useful and the St John Ambulance Brigade regularly runs courses in many towns. In a large walking group it is always desirable to have at least one trained first aider out on a ramble.

FIRST AID KIT

It is sensible, whenever you go walking, to carry a few first aid items with you. A roll of 3 in. crêpe bandage, a packet of adhesive plasters, a pair of scissors and a tube of antiseptic cream would be fine for dealing with the most common emergencies. They cost little and are easy to pop into a rucksack. A few triangular bandages could also be useful, though in an emergency they can be improvised with items of clothing.

BLISTERS

Newcomers to rambling often get a few blisters until their feet have become properly hardened, though even seasoned walkers may suffer the occasional one, especially when breaking in new boots. Blisters are not usually a serious problem but are painful and can take away the pleasure of a day's outing. Most regular walkers have at some time or another come across a group of young people spending a few days walking as part of the Duke of Edinburgh's Award Scheme, and it is quite common to find that one or two are in trouble from blisters. All credit to them that they don't give up — but better not to have the blisters in the first place.

Prevention is always better than cure, so don't plunge into a long walk until you are sure that your feet and your boots are happy with each other. Make certain that your boots are a good fit before you buy them and that they are properly broken in. Modern boots are, in fact, much easier to break in than those of a few years ago, but, even so, use them for a few short walks at first.

Be careful when you put your socks on to see that you don't get any creases in them — rucked socks are the quickest way to get blisters. Watch out, too, to make sure that any darns are not going to produce the same results.

If you feel a sore patch developing on your foot stop and attend to it at once. A plaster put on the sore area will stop a blister from forming. If one does develop before you become aware of it, and you still have several miles to walk, the only remedy is to pop it. To do this you need a sterilised needle, pin or blade. A match or cigarette lighter can be used to heat the needle to the point of redness. Prick the edge of the blister to release the fluid, then dab on antiseptic cream and cover with a plaster.

BEE AND WASP STINGS

Bee and wasp stings are always unpleasant but not fatal unless you happen to be one of the very rare people with an allergy to the poison. Wasp stings are best treated with vinegar, but if you don't have that on a ramble you can perhaps use lemon or orange juice.

Bees, unlike wasps, leave their sting in your skin. Don't be tempted to try to pull one out because this will squeeze in more venom. Work it gently free with a sterilised needle or pin. Bicarbonate of soda solution will help to relieve the pain, but if this is not available use antiseptic or anti-histamine cream.

Stings in the mouth can be dangerous if the tongue swells and closes off airways. The only thing to do is to try to reduce the swelling with mouthfuls of cold water and cold compresses around the neck. Medical attention must be sent for urgently.

SNAKE BITES

There is only one poisonous snake in Britain, the viper or adder. Its bite is not fatal to a normal healthy adult though anyone bitten should stay calm and not rush about as this simply circulates the poison faster. The affected limb will swell up after about fifteen minutes and become painful. An anti-snake bite injection is desirable — usually only obtainable from a hospital. Children are likely to be more affected than adults so prompt medical aid for them is important.

OTHER BITES

The end of a warm dry day is the time when gnats and midges can descend on you in clouds. The effect of their bites, like those of the horsefly, tends to be delayed action and they become itchy some time after the little blighters have had their fill of blood. Again, prevention is better than cure, so if you have remembered to dab on some insect repellant you might escape. Otherwise, all that you can do is to use some antiseptic or anti-histamine cream and try not to scratch. Midges are an especial nuisance in parts of Scotland in the summer months.

ANKLE SPRAINS

If you sprain an ankle stop at once to treat it. Unless it is too painful, take off the boot and bathe the foot and ankle in a stream, pond or any available cold water. This will help to prevent or reduce swelling. If the sprain appears to be severe and accompanied by great pain, leave the boot on but plunge the lot into cold water if that is possible.

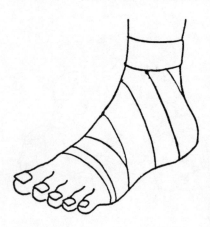

Bracing a sprain.

Then use a bandage to strap up the ankle. Pull the bandage round the site of the sprain (usually the outside joint), then go around the ankle above the injury. This will help to brace the ankle and you may be able to continue, carefully. If the sprain is too bad for you to stand, stay seated and send for help. If you are in doubt about whether it is a sprain or a fracture, always treat it as a fracture. Stay still and get help.

SPRAINED TOES

It is possible to sprain a toe joint when you accidentally stub a toe or trip over rocks on a steep incline. All sprains take time to heal and really need medical attention, but out in the countryside you must be your own doctor for temporary measures. Take off your boot and dip the toe in cold water if possible, or put wet, cold compresses round the joint to prevent or reduce swelling. Do not continue walking if in great pain, sit still and send for help.

NOSE BLEED

A nose bleed is not uncommon but on a walk can be distressing, so know how to deal with it. Squeeze gently the soft part of the nose between finger and thumb for about ten minutes. This will allow a blood clot to form and so stop the flow. It is useless and dangerous to plug the nostrils with cotton wool without first stopping the bleeding.

HEAT EXHAUSTION

Although more commonly met in tropical countries a sudden and unexpected hot spell in an otherwise cool summer can sometimes result in the unwary rambler suffering from heat exhaustion (sometimes known as heat stroke). Direct sunlight beating down can cause an excessive loss of body fluid through sweating, and that can result in the body temperature going dangerously high. The first sign may be leg cramps and a feeling of illness and exhaustion followed, sometimes, by fainting or vomiting.

The stricken person should stop walking, seek the shade and drink plenty of cool liquid — in sips not gulps. A little salt should be taken if possible — about half a teaspoonful in a pint of water. Then try to get the body temperature down by cold water swabs to the head and body. Remove excessive clothing. Give plenty of time for the victim to recover before moving off — but the walk should be abandoned in case the problem recurs. If the symptons persist medical help should be sent for urgently.

To avoid heat exhaustion wear a hat and cool clothes and always carry enough to drink. Pack some salt tablets, available from pharmacists and outdoor shops, if you think that the weather is going to be exceptionally hot. Drink plenty of water and if you develop signs of exhaustion don't hesitate to rest up for a few hours until it is cooler. If you are susceptible to this condition avoid hills, mountains and hard walking in the hottest part of the day.

HYPOTHERMIA

Hypothermia is more commonly associated with the elderly during the coldest parts of winter. It might therefore surprise you to learn that young people caught out in the hills and mountains die faster from this condition than old people do inside their unheated homes. All that is required is a cold, wet, windy day — familiar conditions to anyone walking in Britain!

"I think he's starting to thaw out."

Hypothermia is difficult to spot at first. The victim will feel cold and tired. Speech may be affected and behaviour may become erratic or aggressive. This stage can be followed by lethargy, cramp, violent shivering and death.

The victim must stop walking at once and speedy efforts must be made to find immediate shelter, especially from the wind which is the real killer — remember the chill factor described in chapter 8. However, if there is no shelter close by, don't carry on walking in the hope of finding some. Just stop where you are — erect a tent if you have one with you. Hypothermia needs urgent attention so send off some of the fittest members of the group in search of help.

Do everything possible to keep the victim warm with extra clothing or, indeed, anything suitable that you are carrying. Remember that heat can be lost to the cold ground so insulate underneath as well as on top. Put the victim inside a sleeping bag or plastic survival bag if you have one, preferably accompanied by a fit member of the party to provide extra warmth. If the victim is conscious give warm drinks and energy rich foods such as chocolate, sweets and dried fruit. Never give brandy or any alcohol which can have the opposite to the desired effect — so much for the St. Bernard dog ploughing through the snow! Don't rub the victim's skin or use a hot water bottle — this can simply cause cold blood to rush to the heart or other parts of the body.

Remember that if one member of a party has been affected others also may succumb. So every member of the party should watch out for symptoms in their companions.

Like most ills hypothermia is preventable, either by taking enough clothes and equipment, or by not tackling mountain walks when the weather is wet and windy, or seems likely to become so. Always go adequately clothed (jeans are not suitable wear) and have extra warm clothing with you, even when weather conditions seem ideal. They can change quite unpredictably. Use local weather forecasts to find out what conditions are likely.

Have a good breakfast and carry a supply of energy producing foods. A plastic survival bag should be an essential item of equipment.

The author, like many ramblers, has several times come across young people high in the hills who are totally unprepared for the cold. They are seen in everyday clothes, jeans and trainers, and never give hypothermia a thought. It shouldn't happen to you now, should it?

FROSTNIP AND FROSTBITE

If hands, feet and face are not adequately protected in cold weather they can be affected by frostnip. The opening symptoms are these parts feeling very cold and then very painful. The next stage is numbness, and then, if it becomes worse, frostbite.

Two pairs of woollen socks, warm clothes, thermal gloves or mitts will help to prevent frostnip of fingers and toes. A hat and a well laced up anorak hood will protect the head.

Anyone whose hands are affected should put them underneath their clothes, preferably under their armpits or between their legs. Immersion in warm water will also help if there is any available. Feet, if possible, are best placed on a companion's stomach and well covered with clothing, plastic bags, towels or whatever. Do not rub the skin because body cells that have frozen may become infected by the friction. Seek medical attention and never allow the victim to soldier bravely on — this can cause even more problems.

"That should reduce his temperature!"

BLEEDING

It is difficult to avoid the occasional cut when rambling, usually caused by barbed wire, nails in fences, thorns or undergrowth. Treatment is simple. If there is a lot of blood use a sterile bandage to make a pad and then hold this over the wound until bleeding stops. A small wound should soon stop — a deeper one might take ten minutes. When the bleeding has stopped make a triangular bandage out of any material available to hold the pad in place. Small wounds can be covered with a plaster.

YOUR FEET

The human foot is a marvellous piece of mechanism. It has twenty-six bones arranged in arches to take your weight, allow you to walk, run, jump or stand still. Most of us come into the world with perfect feet so why are foot problems so common? It's not our fault of course. We just grew that way for a variety of reasons — poor shoes when small, badly fitted army boots when older, too much standing about, not enough walking, and so on. But as we have only one pair for life we ought to look after them.

When your feet give trouble you can hurt all over, with pains in your legs and even back ache. We can strengthen our feet by exercises; easy ones such as rising up and down on the toes, clenching them, stretching out the feet, circling them and, of course, washing them daily. Encasing feet in shoes for long periods provides ideal conditions for the growth of fungi and bacteria — we don't want smelly feet do we?

Toe nails should always be cut straight, not rounded, to prevent ingrowing toe nails. Corns and callouses need to be removed regularly.

Feet were designed for walking with toes straight ahead. In fact many of us have slightly splayed out feet, and some are pigeon-toed. Our feet seem to compensate for mistakes in gait. Try to cultivate a good walking style with your feet straight — it's sometimes hard but never too late to change.

TETANUS

It is wise for everyone to have a tetanus injection at least every five years. See your GP about this. Tetanus (also commonly known as lockjaw) is always very unpleasant, and sometimes fatal, despite modern medicine. It is always a risk after a wound, especially if it has been contaminated with soil. A tetanus injection is particularly important after a dog bite.

SUNBURN

You can easily become sunburnt when out walking on a sunny day — and it need not be high summer. Indeed sunburn is very common at the beginning of a warm spell. Nylon shirts or blouses may give the impression of protection but this is not so — the harmful ultra-violet rays from the sun can easily penetrate such clothing.

You should always protect exposed areas (not forgetting your face and neck) with a good anti-sunburn cream or lotion. These are now graded according to the degree of protection that they provide. Always use a high protection (no. 6 or higher) grade, at least until you have acquired a good tan. Excessive and unprotected exposure to the sun can cause skin cancer.

Bad burns need expert medical attention. Gently bathing burns in cold water will reduce the skin temperature and bring some relief.

OTHER EMERGENCIES ...

There are, of course, all sorts of illnesses that can attack ramblers out in the countryside, just as they can when they are at home or in the street. However, an untrained first aider can do more harm than good so I feel it best to leave mention of emergencies such as asthma attacks or heart attacks out of this book. Everyone can benefit from good first aid training whatever their occupation or activity.

In cases of misfortune that you don't know how to deal with, the best thing is to make the victim comfortable, try to reassure, and seek urgent medical help.

But it should be emphasised that the great majority of ramblers don't experience illness or a major accident when they are out. Indeed, they generally comprise the healthier section of the population through regular and moderately strenuous exercise. Take heart from this and don't worry when you are out — just be prepared.

11

Be a Leader

Any ramble involving more than one person requires a leader. Unless you are following a simple, short and clearly defined route there are going to be occasions when some decision making will be required, either during the walk or before you set out. So this chapter is about leadership and what is involved when you find yourself in this position.

ROUTE SELECTION

This, of course, must come first. If you already know the proposed area well you may be able to work out a route quickly using the appropriate OS map or maps. Remember that the 1:25000 Pathfinder series maps are much more informative and easier to read than the 1:50000 series, the presence of field boundaries being particularly helpful. Keep as far as possible off roads which may be hazardous if busy, and always hard on the feet.

If you intend to walk in an unfamiliar area then collect together the appropriate maps (you can usually borrow these from the larger public libraries), but don't imagine that you will necessarily be able to work out a route from them. As I have mentioned earlier, the presence of a right of way on a map does not necessarily mean that it will be walkable. Paths may have disappeared, stiles or gates blocked, byways become completely overgrown.

It is better, if you can, to visit your library or bookseller and borrow or buy a book of walks covering the area of interest. You don't have to slavishly follow the routes described but at least you can take advantage of the fact that someone has already done some investigation into the state of the local paths. Even so, don't take everything that you read as gospel. A route may be perfectly clear when the author last walked it but that may have been some years ago. Look at the date of publication of the book and if it is several years old be especially on the look out for recent changes on the ground. But, even so, some sudden changes may have occurred affecting even a recently published book. And, whatever the book says, always have good OS maps with you. Never rely entirely on maps published in walking guides. Many are excellent, but mistakes are not unknown. And a simple route map may be of no help if you want to break off your walk and make your way to the nearest pub, bus stop, railway station or hospital.

"Do something — you're the leader!"

Think carefully about how far you want to walk, bearing in mind the capabilities of your party. Remember that a party can only go as fast as its slowest member. Check how many stiles there are to climb over — a lot of these will slow the party down quite considerably. If there are hills on the walk remember that the average speed will be reduced. Use Naismith's rule:'For ordinary walking allow one hour for every three miles on the map plus an additional hour for every 2,000 feet climbed.' The height climbed is not the highest point reached but the sum of all the separate ascents which, on some walks, can be numerous. Allow extra time for difficult terrain, bad weather, loo stops and meal stops. Remember that steep descents can sometimes prove more difficult and taxing on the feet and legs than ascents.

RECONNOITRE

Ii is normally essential to do a preliminary reconnaissance before taking a party out. You will learn exactly where you are going, how far it will be, how difficult the walking will be, and you can plan your stops. It is helpful to have a companion with you. Be prepared to have to make on the spot amendments to the proposed route. If you find obstructions these can be reported to the local Highway Authority — but don't expect that the obstructions will necessarily have been removed before you do your walk.

"This is the jump or swim bit."

Then draw up a brief list of information for your party:

1. Name and place of starting point, with map grid reference if the members of the party have to make their own way there.
2. Mileage.
3. Grade of walking — easy, moderate, strenuous.
4. Exact time of departure and expected time of return.
5. Lunch stop. Can food be obtained at a pub or café? Will you be allowed to eat sandwiches in the pub?

"Yes, I think we're near the pub stop."

6. Transport details — coach, car or public transport. If the latter give departure times, alighting point, train route or bus service number.
7. Will dogs be allowed?
8. Your own telephone number or address.

If your ramble is open to the general public, this information should go to the local press and radio well in advance, together with details of what to wear.

TRANSPORT

Decide on the starting and finishing points of the walk bearing in mind the mode of transport to be used. Are there suitable car parks or can cars safely be left beside the road? If it is not a circular walk will some cars have to be left at the end of the walk? — if so, extra time will be required at the start of the walk to get them there. If you are going to be a large group using a coach remember that whereas a car might safely be left beside a road, a coach in the same place could cause a serious obstruction.

If public transport is to be used, carefully check timetables and make certain that yours are up to date. Telephone the bus company or railway station a few days before the walk to confirm your times.

LUNCH STOPS

Arrange where you are going to stop for lunch, for rest breaks and for loo stops. If lunch is going to be taken, picnic style, in the countryside pick a sheltered spot in case of bad weather. If in a village pub enquire in advance if members of the party can eat their own sandwiches in the pub or, if not, in the pub garden. Some publicans rely greatly on their food trade and so may, understandably, not want you to bring your own. Be reasonable if this is the case — the publican has his living to make.

Find out what food is on offer and let your group know in good time. Publicans are usually most helpful to ramblers who, after all, bring quite a lot of custom to them — but, if you are going to be more than a small family group, always let them know of your proposed visit. Sometimes publicans will put a room or bar at the disposal of a good sized party. If the walking has been muddy get the party to clean up their boots as well as possible before going inside the premises. Leave boots outside if the publican has a rooted objection to mud on the carpets. If everyone carries plastic bags with them that can solve the problem at a stroke.

Always let your party know at what time you propose to leave the pub, otherwise some thirsty walkers might take some getting out!

REST STOPS

How many rests that you have will depend much on the composition of the party and the length of the walk. A B-party might expect several short stops in a walk of eight to ten miles. An A-party might happily keep going except for refreshment stops and loo stops. It is usual to have a morning and an afternoon stop for refreshment — many walkers will carry a flask of tea or coffee for this purpose. If it is very hot a few more stops may be needed to avoid getting dehydrated.

If the party is prone to becoming spread out (especially likely if it is a large one) you must make periodic stops to allow everyone to catch up. It does nothing for your reputation if you loose half your party!

LOO STOPS

Public loos are not commonly encountered in the countryside so, if you are leading a party, you will need to anticipate calls of nature and plan for these when you are planning the walk. The usual procedure is for the leader to bring the party to a halt at a suitable stop and then announce 'men forward' or 'ladies forward'. The party can then split in two and join up again when nature has been satisfied.

Always have at least two loo stops, one mid-morning (or soon after starting if you have had a long journey) and one early afternoon — not more than half an hour after lunch if you have stopped at a pub. More stops will be needed if your walk is a particularly lengthy one, and more on a cold day than on a very hot one.

"We've only lost three so far."

ON THE DAY

Remember that as leader you are responsible for the party, for keeping it together and for making sure that no-one gets lost. Always carry a first aid kit with you or make sure that someone in the party has one. If you are walking in the mountains get a weather forecast before you leave home (see chapter 16).

Give your party a friendly welcome, paying particular attention to any newcomers. Check on car parking. If you allow dogs, make certain that they are on leads. See that each walker is properly clothed and equipped and, if the walk is to be a strenuous one, exclude anyone who is likely to be a danger to themselves and to others.

If you are leading a coach ramble make quite certain that your driver knows precisely where you are to be picked up and what time you expect to arrive.

Give a brief chat about the walk, describing any particularly interesting features, the distance, any hills or difficult terrain, and where you going to stop for lunch. Have a careful head count before you start, check numbers periodically during the walk and always again at the end.

If possible appoint a back marker, someone experienced, who can close gates and keep a check on stragglers. Expect your party to become spaced out, especially if it is a large one and you encounter lots of stiles. Don't let it get too long or you will risk losing some members. Try to keep a steady pace that will suit the slower walkers. This will probably be less than your usual pace.

A long party is most likely to get split where a path forks, especially if this is in woodland. The trick here, and on winding paths, is to ask members of the party to hang back at such points until those following can see which way to go. But this won't work if the party gets too strung out. Also, remind walkers that if, at any time, they have quite lost sight of people who should be following behind they should pass a message forward to stop the leader.

12

Walking Holidays

If you like company, with everything laid on, then organised walking holidays are for you. There are a number of organisations in Britain catering for walkers of all ages and abilities. Single folk, families and groups are all welcome — and many return year after year.

Organised holidays have many advantages. Walks are carefully planned and led by experienced leaders. You don't have to worry about food which is supplied in plenty before, during and after a walk. Accommodation is usually good as is the

service and surroundings. It's possible to meet a twin soul on a walking holiday, and you will almost certainly find other people who share your interests. One of the nicest things about these breaks is the chance to make new friends who will be remembered long after the holiday is over.

HOME OR AWAY?

Walking holidays are neither particularly cheap nor excessively expensive, but they are usually very good value for money. There are so many first class holidays to choose from that the difficulty is confining yourself to only one.

You could go to the romantic places that you have long fancied; to the hills and mountains that have beckoned you; along the shores of lake and sea in Europe; to Nepal, Peru, China, and many other exciting places.

If you are a home bird, Britain would take a lifetime to walk and explore properly. There is no risk of running out of places to visit.

EASY OR TOUGH?

Most walking holidays provide several grades of walk which can vary between a few miles and strenuous, long mountain treks for which you need to be particularly fit and have a good head for heights. You should be realistic about how fit and active you are, and be sure that children, if you have them, are old enough and fit enough for the difffferent levels of walking. It's no fun to tag onto a group who bat along at a fast rate while you are gasping for breath two miles behind. Mountains are sometimes harder than they look, and it's not a good feeling to look up to distant peaks and see the group you are meant to be with waving down to you. Pick the right walk for you; one that is neither too difficult nor too easy. If you are at all in doubt always consult the leader before setting out. If you are out of practice start with the shorter walks and gradually increase to the longer ones: this is the commonsense way of building up your capacity and stamina.

But don't be put off hill walking, because there is something magic about reaching the summit of a high place and looking down — a magic that can be only experienced but not described.

Among the advantages of rambling holidays in Britain are: no language difficulties, other than possibly strange dialects; no currency problems, other than a shortage of same; and the food will usually be of a kind known to our stomachs — there's no fun finding the the local stewed goat has disagreed with you when you are half-way up Everest. And if things get too much one can smartly head for home.

HF Holidays Ltd. offer a hundred walking holidays in Britain, for all ages and abilities, based in seventeen country and coastal houses. The graded walks include some of the finest walking regions of the country.

The HF country houses are excellent bases for both rambles and for special activity holidays. There is plenty of good food, accommodation, and leaders for all events. A good pointer to the success of these holidays is the large number of guests who go back year after year. HF Holidays also have rambling groups in many large

94

towns so folk who have been on holidays can meet up and make more friends. My local group, for example, has around 500 members; and an average of three rambles a week are arranged plus occasional social functions.

The Countrywide Holidays Association (CHA) also have thousands of members and have city groups similar to HF. They are an experienced walking and activity holiday organisation with fourteen country and coastal guest houses. Like HF, each centre offers a choice of graded walks led by experienced guides. Holidays are characterised by a houseparty atmosphere with an evening social programme.

Both HF Holidays and CHA also have a programme of walking holidays overseas.

Ramblers' Holidays Ltd. are another good company, catering solely for walkers with an ever increasing overseas holiday programme. They have one week walking tours in Mallorca in the winter, for instance, and offer adventure walking all over the world. On some rambles they arrange for baggage to be transported ahead, so leaving the walker free of everything except his needs for the day.

95

Holidays abroad are more costly of course, but include air fares, leadership, accommodation and well organised walks that may satisfy your wanderlust for a while. There is the perk of being able to pick a place with a good sunshine record, or one that has a predictable climate — the Sahara Desert, the Arctic Circle, the Amazon Forest, to name but three. You could go on a fifteen mile per day ramble in the High Atlas Mountains or a walk on the Jade Mountains in China. The world has shrunk for walkers and there is an almost infinite variety of choice.

There are many other companies who specialise in providing walking holidays both at home and overseas. You will find them advertised in the walking magazines such as *The Rambler* where you will also sometimes find them reported on. Now that walking has become one of the most popular of pastimes we can expect to find more small companies blossoming to cater for the crunch of walking feet.

TREAT BOTH ENDS

If you enjoy both walking and learning you might consider giving your feet and head a treat at the same time. The Field Studies Council organises dozens of courses that involve walking.

You can, for example, ramble round the Wrekin, study the geology of Shropshire or the ecology of the Pembrokeshire Coast. You could go for gentle walks in Borderland country, explore the River Severn, or find out how the Snowdon National Park is managed. You can even spend a weekend studying the ecology of a cow pat which provides one of the finest available examples of animal succession.

The Council has a huge range of courses, with houses in many parts of Britain. The cost of a course, which may be a week or a weekend, includes board, lodging, library, laboratory, transport and other facilities. The tutors and leaders are first class.

Like rambling holidays these courses attract people with like interests and it is easy for the single person to fit in. Many ramblers find that these courses provide an ideal opportunity to learn about the geology and the natural history of their favourite walking areas, so enhancing their future outings.

Field Studies Council courses cater for students of all ages. Many A-level pupils have improved their examination prospects by attending: at the other end of the age scale are pensioners who actively take part year after year.

DO IT YOURSELF

Organised holidays are fine, but you may prefer a walking holiday just with your family or with a small group of friends. Sitting down with your maps to plan a week's walking is a fine activity for a cold winter evening. You can pick a good centre to stay at and go out for day walks, or arrange a continuous walking tour, staying in a different place every night. Unless you are going out of season it is sensible to have all your accommodation booked well in advance.

For a walking tour, a long distance footpath — or part of one — will often be easy to plan because most are well supplied with bed and breakfast accommodation. One of the best sources of information is *The Rambler's Yearbook* published annually by the Ramblers' Association — free to members. National Parks also publish accommodation lists, and Tourist Information Centres have details of accommodation available in their areas. Membership of the Youth Hostels Association will gain you access to 264 hostels in England and Wales, and 78 hostels in Scotland (in addition to hostels throughout the world).

The Rambler's Yearbook lists recommended guest houses, farms, hotels and private accommodation. It also contains much other useful material, including information about Long Distance Paths, best buys in walking equipment, and public transport services.

The easiest and quickest way to book up your accommodation is by telephone. If the place that you are telephoning cannot take you, and there is nowhere else listed in the Yearbook, ask if they can give you the address and telephone number of somebody nearby. Almost always there is somebody else around who will provide bed and breakfast.

Many places will provide an evening meal when you arrive and a packed lunch on the following day. It is sensible to arrange these when you telephone.

Always confirm your booking promptly by letter and send a deposit.

If you are moving on to a new place each day you will have to think very carefully about what you take with you. Your luggage will have to go on your back, unless you have a member of the family or group who prefers motoring to walking and will daily transport everything for you.

Unless you are a commando type you should limit what you carry to about 25 lbs. Some backpackers, with camping and cooking gear and food, manage twice this, but most walkers prefer to avoid such feats of endurance. Think very carefully about what you need to have with you. As well as what you would carry on a day walk you will need extra clothing and toilet materials. Consider every unnecessary ounce — these could add up to unnecessary pounds. Put everything together a few days before you leave and weigh it on the bathroom scales. Almost certainly it will come to about 50 lbs! Then you have the fun of deciding what to discard.

You might be able to do some washing en route, though drying could be difficult. Better, before you leave, to post some clean clothes to the mid-address on your walk, then post your discarded clothes home — or to a kindly relative who will wash them. A two-day stop about half-way through your holiday will provide an opportunity for washing, mending, repair to blisters and general recuperation.

If you are new to backpacking have a few practice walks with your rucksack packed to the weight you are going to carry — a pile of books will soon bring it up to the 25 lb figure. Make these full day walks and about as strenuous as those that you going to be doing on your tour.

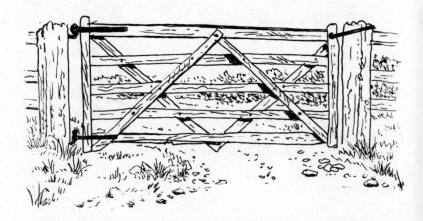

13
Wildlife

If you are a city dweller your experience of wildlife may well be restricted to what you have observed at all night parties or disco rave ups. But when you get out into the country you have a wonderful opportunity to see many wild creatures in their

Red Deer

natural habitat. So this chapter is for those who want to be able to recognise and to know something about some of the animals they are likely to meet.

DEER

The red deer is the largest British mammal and can be seen in the wild, in parks, in reserves, on deer farms, and moors such as Exmoor. The stag reaches peak condition for the autumn rut when he will round up as many females as he can and fight off rivals. At this time he is aggressive and has been known to charge at man. Before charging there are warning signals; the deer will roar or bark, paw the ground and then charge. Often it can be a mock charge, but walkers should not take chances and should avoid venturing onto a stag's territory at this time. Fallow, sika and muntjac stags are similarly smitten when in rut.

Fallow Deer

Red deer like forests and mountain edges. Those kept in parks and reserves grow to be better specimens than those found in the wild Scottish highlands. Though the majority of ramblers seem to be against blood sports it should be pointed out that the red deer would probably have disappeared long ago but for the people who hunt them. These beautiful animals can cause havoc to crops but are conserved for the hunt.

Fallow deer are recognised by their palmated (flattened out) antlers and spotted coats. The truly wild ones are very nervous and will stand still behind trees and watch

100

walkers, who seldom know that they are being observed. Sometimes just the twitch of an ear can be seen. They feed at dawn and dusk and may be spotted gliding through the forest like pale shadows.

Young deer are born in June or July and are most appealing, but if found they should never be picked up. To do so would be to condemn them to death — the mother will abandon her young if she smells man's scent on them.

Roe Deer

The little roe deer has great power to multiply if conditions are right. It prefers cover in conifer plantations which, in recent years, has been provided in plenty by the Forestry Commission. Although it is now quite common it is not often seen because it hides from man — and if it is going to be shot who can blame it? The roe is about the size of a big dog but moves very quickly. Like other deer it likes to feed at dawn and dusk but is sometimes seen grazing during the day.

HEDGEHOGS NEED HELP

The humble, well liked, hedgehog is frequently encountered, alas, as a squashed blob on the road. It is the hedgehog's response to vibrations which cause it to roll up before oncoming cars and lorries. It has poor vision but good other senses. Walkers often hear these delightful animals as they trundle through undergrowth and along hedgerows in search of food.

The hedgehog can run, climb and swim, but many fall into cattle grids and starve unless helped out. To this end the British Hedgehog Preservation Society provide exit ramps for them in some parts of the country. Ramblers, kind folk that they are, can also help to rescue any trapped animals. You can pick them up wearing gloves, or even without if you hold them gently. They are not heavy so light pressure by the hands does no harm and you should not get pricked by the spines. Alternatively lift them up by sliding a forked branch underneath, or use a coat or a piece of other material.

Be warned that hedgehogs have dozens of fleas swarming through their spines — but these fleas won't live on humans.

MOLES

Few ramblers actually see moles but everyone notices molehills which are the spoil heaps from tunnel digging. Rarely, a mole might be seen pushing up a mound of soil, or disappearing into the ground. It can dig out of sight in thirty seconds in soft soil and three minutes in heavy clay.

Adult moles prefer broad-leaved woodland to open meadow. The molehills that you stumble over in open ground are made by young moles who are not allowed into the woods by their fiercely territorial seniors.

BATS NEED SAVING

The tail end of a ramble, when the sun is almost down, is the time to see bats flitting madly about. Contrary to popular belief these creatures are harmless, clean, sociable and intelligent.

Their numbers have declined rapidly in recent years and are now a fraction of what they were a century ago. This is principally due to the widespread use of insecticides which reduce the bats' food supply. Wet summers and the loss of many roosting sites have added to their problems. Ironically, the smallest British bat, the pipistrelle, can take over 3,000 insects in just one night — a feat which must surely make it a better insecticide than any produced by man.

Bats are now, rightly, protected by law and you must not disturb them or destroy them. They roost not only in church belfries but also in the lofts of both old and new houses. Pest controllers who treat timber for wood-boring beetles may unknowingly kill bats — which would eat those beetles!

Lady ramblers need not fear bats flying into their hair. This is an ancient unfounded myth. Bats are too bright to risk injury to delicate wings or to tangle with anything in their direction of flight.

CRAWLY THINGS

VIPERS (ADDERS). Snakes make some people cringe — there seems to be a universal horror of these reptiles. In this country we have the viper, or adder, as our only poisonous snake and it has a reputation that it doesn't deserve. Walkers seldom see one because usually it can't get away from man fast enough. When the weather is cold the viper becomes sluggish and it is then that you might come across one. It is easily recognised by a dark zig-zag pattern down the back. It is quite small — not much longer than twice the length of a walking boot.

If suddenly surprised it will freeze into a stick-like shape and will not attack unless handled, trodden on or disturbed. Most wild creatures defend themselves when threatened.

The bite of a viper is not fatal to a normal healthy adult. The chances of being bitten are about equal to winning a vast fortune on a football pool — pretty remote!

103

As advised in chapter 10 anyone bitten by a viper should stay calm and not rush about, as this simply circulates the poison faster. The affected limb will swell up after about fifteen minutes and become painful. An anti-snake bite injection is desirable — usually only obtainable from a hospital. Children are likely to be more affected than adults so prompt medical aid for them is important.

GRASS SNAKES. The largest British snake is the grass snake which can be over five feet long. It is brown, green or a mixture of both colours and can be distinguished by a yellow or white neck band. It moves very fast and is a good swimmer. It is harmless except to frogs which form its staple diet. As might be expected it is found near to water, marsh or swampy ground. If handled it can emit a nasty smell like bad eggs.

LIZARDS. If you are observant you will come across the pretty, nippy, common lizard on moor, heathland, stone walls and even high up in some mountain regions. It is small — only as large as your index finger — and moves so fast that many people miss it. In the Spring the male lizard displays bright orange or red patches on his stomach. The lizard is on the menu of vipers, birds of prey and other mammals.

SLOW WORMS. The slow worm is badly named. It is actually a legless lizard which looks like a smooth snake and moves like one. It is harmless to man and most useful as it eats a number of pests. Slugs, snails, worms and many insects form its food supply.

If trapped or roughly picked up the slow worm will shed half its tail which will then twist violently about on the ground, distracting its enemy while the slow worm escapes. The tail will regrow in time. Treated gently the creatures may be tamed, but they should not be taken out of their natural environment.

All our British reptiles are declining due to loss of habitat and the use of insecticides which cause a shortage of food for them. If organic farming came to stay our countryside would be that much richer in wildlife.

FURRY THINGS

RABBITS. Farmers and foresters tend to hate the humble rabbit but a sight of this animal always pleases ramblers who watch it scurrying off as they approach. Rabbits doubtless cause much damage to crops and young trees but they also provide man with fur and flesh. Friend big-ears is a most important food supply for fox, stoat, weasel, buzzard, hawk, owl and eagle.

Rabbits keep grass closely cropped and keep down the tall growing varieties which tend to strangle wild flowers. By making patches in open ground they improve the habitat for ants — which are then eaten by green woodpeckers and other birds. Left to itself nature always seems to balance good against bad. Long live this charming little animal!

HARES. Out in the country you will sometimes come across a hare loping effortlessly over field, meadow or up a hill. Bigger than a rabbit it has powerful hind legs which give it thrust when running uphill.

Mink

The expression 'mad as a March hare' refers to the animal's behaviour when seen in the Spring. This performance was once thought of as a form of madness, but this is not so. The male is making a pass at his lady friend who quite often thumps him off. This is the reason for his boxing-like postures which actually start in January and continue right up to July.

MINK. Wild, or feral, mink are almost everywhere now after escaping from fur farms. They are dark brown, almost black, with black tipped tails, and are smaller and lighter than the ranch mink. The ferret-like wild mink is quite ferocious and can only be handled with thick hide gloves.

Mink are deadly predators that take fish, birds, mammals and eggs. They live near water and hole up in thick undergrowth, in hollow trees and under rocks. They can swim, run, jump and climb at an amazing speed. Poultry farmers need to look out when there's a mink about. This bundle of joy is savage and in places upsets the ecological balance.

Grey Squirrel

SQUIRRELS. The grey squirrel is widespread and abundant in town and country. We all see them in parks, gardens and almost anywhere there are a few trees. Given a choice these creatures prefer broad-leaved woodland. They eat acorns, beechmast, hazelnuts and a huge range of other foods, including crops, flower bulbs and seeds. They cause great damage to growing trees, plants and shrubs, and can be devastating to birds eggs and chicks. Even so, this pretty animal is well liked and soon learns to take food from a human hand.

The elusive red squirrel is smaller than the grey and has ear tufts. It is usually found in coniferous forests where it has a constant food supply. Fir cones provide oil-rich seeds for the red squirrel, but it will also eat hazelnut, beechmast and acorns when they are available.

Red Squirrel

You are more likely to see this beautiful animal in the Lake District and in Scotland. It is very localised in England and is thought to be totally absent from many counties.

VOLES. Water voles, commonly (but incorrectly) called water rats can frequently be seen as you ramble along stream, river and canal banks. Sometimes you may just hear a splash. These charming little vegetarian creatures are harmless. Water voles have been known to accept sandwich crumbs.

Bank and field voles will also clear up any food scraps left by ramblers. These rodents are an important food source for all birds of prey and other predatory creatures, as also are field and wood mice.

A JUMPING THING. If you are walking in Derbyshire, and are extraordinarily lucky, you might just see a red-necked wallaby bounding about. These animals, native to Australia, have been wild here for over twenty years. After a few were released from captivity they adapted to the environment and have held on ever since.

WILD CATTLE

Cattle which are descended from animals which were common here in the Bronze Age may be seen at Chillingham (near Berwick-upon-Tweed), Woburn (Bedfordshire), Vaynol (Gwyneth), Dynevor (Dyfed) and Cadzow (Strathclyde). They are impressive animals with white coats and ox-like horns. They are the nearest that we can see to the original wild ox hunted by early man and later domesticated by him.

Highland Cattle can now be seen in many places outside the Highlands. They are a beautiful golden to sandy colour and seem fairly docile. You may come across herds of these or, sometimes, the odd one or two in a farm.

A Chillingham Bull

PONIES

You will meet so-called wild ponies on Dartmoor, Exmoor and in the New Forest. These delightful animals are, in fact, all owned by someone and are rounded up each autumn for marking and sending to market, where they are bought for riding. They are strong, hardy creatures who fend for themselves, and are descended from ponies once used as pack or colliery animals.

Wild ponies stay in family groups for much of the year, but stallions may drift away on their own during the winter.

WILD SHEEP

On the islands of Lundy, Skokholm, Ailsa Crag and St. Kilda there are wild sheep which are the descendants of those farmed by Neolithic man. They are known as Soay sheep — Soay is a Norse word meaning Island of Sheep.

Soay Sheep

These fascinating animals are small and goat-like with dark brown coats which are moulted seasonally. They are very nimble, surefooted and hardy. In winter they will eat seaweed to survive. Soay sheep are now bred in some zoos and, as a result, are becoming better known.

Information about the location of rare breeds can be obtained by sending a stamped addressed envelope to the Rare Breeds Survival Trust (see Appendix).

WILD (FERAL) GOATS

One of the first animals to be domesticated by early man, after the dog, was the goat. It suited man because, like him, it was nomadic, and did not need much looking after. It could survive on the worst of pastures, and still find enough to eat among the rocks.

Today, in a few places, there are herds of wild goats which are the descendants of the original strains. You can come across these in the Snowdon region, the Cheviots, and high up along rocky coastal paths. They tend to have untidy, shaggy coats which may be black, white or a mixture of both. Unlike sheep, goats of both sexes have horns. Some of the rams have a wicked looking pair.

These shy creatures are exceptionally sure-footed and occupy rocky regions. I have seen goats in the Snowdon area jump from rocky ledges into the tops of tall trees to feed off leaves. After eating, they trot along branches and leap back without the slightest trouble. If you meet any doing this be careful how you tell people — they might be somewhat unbelieving and suggest that you spent too much time in the pub at lunchtime!

The kids are born in February. Many die but goats breed rapidly to allow for this. They can do great damage to growing crops and trees and their numbers are kept down by shooting. However, some landowners tolerate them so, thanks to them, they continue to exist in the wild.

FEATHERED FRIENDS

Birds are the most commonly seen wildlife creatures. Most ramblers will have watched a heron hunting along a stream or river, a buzzard soaring high in the sky on a thermal of warm air, a kestrel hovering over hedgerow or meadow. And the lucky few will have had the sight of a magnificent golden eagle wheeling over mountain tops.

Along rivers, streams and canals you might glimpse the blue flash of a kingfisher, or watch a brown, black and white bird called a dipper. This bird is remarkable for the way it can walk under water to catch aquatic insects. Sadly its numbers are declining from poisoning by insecticides. The bobbing tail of a grey, yellow or pied wagtail is often seen, and you will meet many sorts of water fowl.

In broad-leaved forests we can hear the mocking laugh-like call of the green woodpecker or the peculiar cha-cha noise that the great spotted woodpecker makes as it nervously watches our approach. Birds feel threatened by movement and clatter so we are more likely to hear than see the singers.

The little owl, about the size of a thrush, can be seen during the day as it hunts over meadow for vole, mice and insects. It likes to perch on top of a post or telegraph pole where you can easily spot it. Another owl sometimes seen by day is the barn owl. It looks mostly white but has a speckled, buff back. This rare bird of prey is a victim to traffic due to its habit of swooping slowly across a road or motorway. It has declined because of loss of its breeding habitat and the use of pesticides.

You may sometimes meet the tawny owl, usually asleep or dozing in a tree. At times it is mobbed by small birds, so drawing our attention to it. It is brown in colour, but viewed at close quarters the feathers are beautifully mottled in shades of brown, buff and white. It used to be common in most towns but the loss of many old trees, the use of pesticides and general pollution has caused its decline. In the wild we hear it hooting as the sun goes down. Like other owls it has down on the underside of its wings which give it silent flight — essential if it is to catch mice, voles and other small creatures which have acute hearing.

The Golden Eagle

Britain is blessed with a great variety of small birds. They can often be hard to recognise at first but there are a number of pocket guides that can be purchased which will greatly help. Expertise comes with practice — rambling friends will greatly appreciate your pointing out the less common species to them. The Royal Society for the Protection of Birds maintain a number of fine bird reserves which you might like to visit on your rambles.

The GOLDEN EAGLE. If you get a chance to visit the island of Skye not only will you have an opportunity for some wonderful walks but also the chance of watching that most majestic of all birds, the golden eagle. Skye has one of the best eagle colonies in Europe. Golden eagles are also found in the Scottish Highlands and, rarely now, in the Lake District. Young eagles may sometimes venture to other parts of the country but there is no evidence that they breed there.

Golden eagles pair for life. In spite of being a protected species they are still shot, trapped or poisoned. They can have a wingspan of seven feet and feed on hare, rabbit, grouse, ptarmigan and fresh carrion. Some sheep farmers maintain that they take new born lambs, but the evidence is that they take only weak, ill or dead ones. Fast drivers kill more sheep than golden eagles but they don't get shot for it!

The golden eagle has wonderful eyesight and can see its prey from a mile high in the sky. It plunges down to earth at ninety miles an hour.

THE WILDLIFE AND COUNTRYSIDE ACT, 1981.

Under this Act it is now an offence to kill, injure or take any wild bird, and to take, destroy or damage the nest or egg of any wild bird. It is also an offence to be in possession of a nest, egg or any part derived from a wild bird.

Deer, seal and badger are protected or partially protected. The Act closely defines the persons who may be entitled to kill such animals. Even some creatures regarded as vermin may only be killed by authorised persons.

There are more than sixty species of plant which may not be picked, uprooted or destroyed. The Act also protects wild fruit which legally belongs to the landowner. Most ramblers, however, are tempted to pick blackberries along their way. This seems to be all right so long as the bushes flank the footpath or byway.

Snakes, lizards and newts are also protected.

If you want a complete list of protected species you can write (enclosing SAE) for this to either the Nature Conservancy Council or the Council for Environmental Conservation.

14

Rambling Plus

To many ramblers the pleasure of being out in the countryside or the mountains is sufficient in itself. But, if you are so inclined, the hours spent out of doors can also be used to develop, or continue, other skills or hobbies. I have frequently been shamed by walking companions who could correctly name every wild flower and tree. One time there was a lady who could identify almost every insect buzzing about — no mean feat when there are thousands of the little blighters.

PHOTOGRAPHY

An automatic camera is easy to handle and useful to carry with you on rambles. You can keep a photographic record of your walks, your walking companions and places of special interest. Building up a series of photographs on a particular theme can become an absorbing hobby — some possible themes are village inns, pub signs, old churches, follies, trig points.

If you want to be more ambitious you could opt for a 35mm reflex camera. If you don't mind the extra weight your system could include zoom and a wide angle lens. A close-up lens is useful for nature shots of flowers, plants and insects. But remember that the pounds do add up and you might not be so enthusiastic for all these extras after a day's slog in the mountains.

You have the choice of slides or prints. Prints are easier to handle and to pass around your friends. Slides will usually give you much better picture quality although involve the complication of a projector and a screen. Slides are useful should you be asked to give a talk on rambling or on your walking experiences. Rambling groups often have a photo evening as a winter social occasion.

ART AS YOU GO

Some ramblers are of an artistic bent and usually carry a sketch pad with them when they are out walking. During rest and lunch breaks it is possible to do some fast drawing. There are many different subjects — fellow walkers, old cottages, churches, farm animals, landscapes.

A soft pencil, eraser and sketch pad are the basic needs, but you could take watercolour or oil crayons which can give quick, fresh studies.

Trees are a wonderful subject for the artist, particularly in winter when branches can be seen in fascinating shapes and compositions. Winter scenes can be as beautiful, and often more dramatic, than those done at other times of the year. Quick drawings of cloud formations are interesting and can be used at a later date as backgrounds to more ambitious pictures. Nature sketches of wild flowers, leaf details, plants and bark are all very interesting and sometimes valuable for future use.

115

Drawing cartoons of fellow ramblers can be great fun. You should spend more time looking at the victim than actually drawing — though you need to learn to observe people properly. This aspect of art is vital for good results. It is wise to draw people when they are unaware of what you are doing, otherwise they may become self-conscious and not look their natural selves.

In fact, drawing cartoons of fellow ramblers led to the birth of this book. You too might meet up with a rambling publisher with a sense of humour who will make a fortune for you. (Publisher's note: Don't be too sure of this!)

RECORD YOUR PROGRESS

Some walkers like to keep a written record of each walk, logging the route, distance, weather, terrain and, sometimes, the brand of beer sold at the village pub.

These notes can be interesting, not only to you in future years, but to family, friends, and, maybe, a future reading public. Brief notes can easily be made as you go along, and a small notebook is no trouble to carry in pocket or rucksack. Accurate records can, perhaps, lead to short articles for your local paper. If you embark on this make sure, in advance, that the paper will pay for your efforts. It could help to finance your future rambles!

If you are artistically inclined a camera is an aid to recording information when you don't have time to get out your sketch map to do a drawing.

BIRDWATCHING

In recent years birdwatching has grown greatly in popularity and there are many inexpensive guides in the bookshops. Many towns have local birdwatching groups. It is an ideal hobby for the rambler who will have ample opportunities to develop the necessary skills of identification. On most rambles it is possible to spot over twenty species of birds, and this can, at times, top forty. On the island of Skomer, for example, over fifty were recorded in a single day.

It is best to start off by trying to recognise the common garden birds that can be seen near your home. This will help you to recognise the various characteristics by which birds are identified in the guides. Even in the middle of a town there is a surprising number of different species.

On your rambles you can maintain a list with date, place, numbers and species of birds seen.

WILDLIFE

Today, thanks to superb TV programmes, people know much more about wildlife than they did twenty years ago. Even so, not everyone can identify all the creatures seen on rambles. But being able to identify the mammals, reptiles, birds and insects that you will meet when you are out will add greatly to the enjoyment of walking. You can then go on to learn more about them, finding out how they live, and what part they play in the ecology of the area. You soon understand what a struggle for survival all wild creatures have, and why and how man is often the worst predator.

BOTANY

Some walkers become expert at recognising wild flowers, fungi, mosses and trees. Once you have become able to recognise what type of tree you are sitting under you can go on to extend your knowledge. What wildlife does the tree support? How long does it live? Does the wood have any economic use? How important is it to the environment?

Again, you will find many pocket guides in your local bookshop. If you have the inclination you could become an amateur David Bellamy in no time!

117

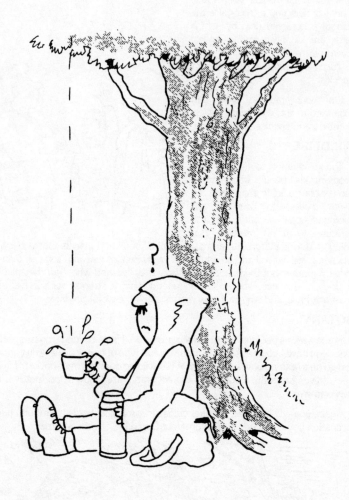

15

To the Woods

One of the great joys of walking in the countryside is looking at trees of different sorts and sizes. Ramblers who explore the Sherwood Forest, for example, can see the magnificent Major Oak which is reported to be between four and five hundred years old. It is 90 feet high with a girth of 33 feet. This ancient oak is older than the legendary Robin Hood and countless thousands of walkers through the ages must have admired its huge branches.

Trees are a vital part of our environment and contribute to all other life. They pump out oxygen during the day and provide food and shelter for many insects, birds and mammals. The leaves which are shed in the autumn fertilize the soil and help to prevent soil erosion. The oak alone supports hundreds of different species, from minute inhabitants of the leaf litter up through a growing food chain to large predators like owls and foxes.

When a mature broad leaved tree is buzz-sawn down in minutes a whole wildlife city is destroyed for good. As we all know, trees in many countries are being cut down to make fast money. But the longer term effects can be catastrophic: soil is eroded and former rain forests can become deserts. A rain forest builds its own weather, and its destruction can result in weather changes on a much wider scale.

In many parts conifers are grown as a cash crop to satisfy the needs of the building and paper industries. Some people think the modern method of growing these is damaging to our environment. Certainly, conifers do not improve the ground or provide food and shelter for many species of bird and animal. Note the sparcity of bird song in a conifer forest compared with that you will hear in a forest containing largely broad leaved trees.

Common Oak

Ironically much of the money put into commercial forestry of this kind comes from the taxpayer. Even the funds of pension schemes are invested in conifer forests. All too often the desire for quick money overshadows the need for a natural countryside.

Hardwood, the world over, is becoming rare and the price of it is going up. At the present time English Oak is worth about £10 per square foot with rarer woods costing much more.

Ramblers can, and do, help the situation by supporting tree preservation causes and the keeping of old woodlands, and by taking care not to damage young trees. Unprotected young trees which have their leading shoots destroyed grow distorted or dwarfed.

HEDGEROWS

Hedgerows, also, are under threat because of modern farming methods supported by Government grants. Since 1947 an incredible 109,000 miles of hedgrows have been destroyed in England, Scotland and Wales, some 22 per cent of the total mileage established over hundreds of years. Hedgerows, like forests, provide an ideal environment for many species of wildlife. More than thirty-five common trees and shrubs can be found in hedges with some 800 species of plants in the verges. Hedges also protect the soil from erosion and help its continuing fertility, as well as contributing greatly to the beauty and variety of the countryside.

HOW TO RECOGNISE TREES

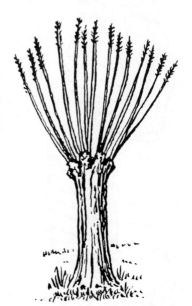

A pollarded willow (winter)

Many ramblers can recognise the common oak because of its size, shape, and the acorns that it produces. The tall poplar and the Christmas tree like fir are well known, but the United Kingdom contains hundreds of other beautiful trees, both native and imported. We have mixed forest, oak woods, coppices, and trees to suit each area. A walk by the river will allow us to see willow, pollard willow (this is the way it is pruned), alder, and others that like plenty of water.

Up in the hills we might come across mountain ash (rowan, as it is commonly known) with, in the autumn, its bunches of vivid red berries. As we wander down lanes we encounter many different kinds of shrub or small tree — hazel, sallow, elder, wayfaring tree, guelder rose, hawthorn and many more. There is a huge variety around us but few of us can recognise more than about half a dozen.

Trees can be classifed roughly into one of three sorts: bushy topped; fir; or poplar type. From this basic shape accurate identification can be made by studying the leaf. The identification can then be confirmed by examination of the trunk and bark. Many of us will recognise the craggy bark of an oak, the white and black patched trunk of a silver birch, the scaly bark of a Scots pine, and maybe the deep red and brown of a wild cherry.

The Scots pine is our only natural pine and some 10,000 years ago much of our land was covered with it. It can be recognised by its height and its reddish brown trunk and upper branches.

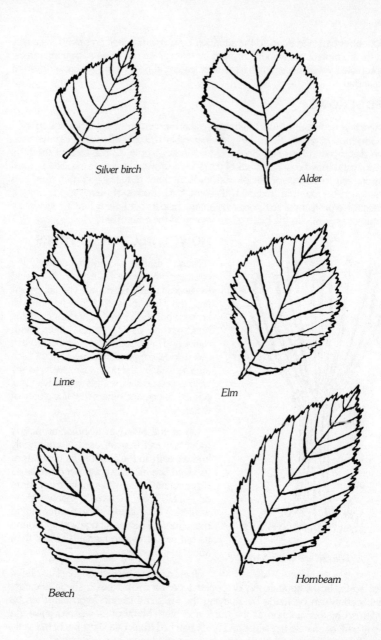

Silver birch

Alder

Lime

Elm

Beech

Hornbeam

As aids to identification, then, we have the general shape, the type of leaf, and the kind of bark to help us. In addition, the many flowering trees, shrubs and bushes can be recognised by their flowers, fruit, nuts and berries. But we still need a good

122

reference book. There are several pocket guides in the bookshops which are ideal for taking on rambles and which will greatly enhance your enjoyment of a day out.

However, you may still come across trees which are not illustrated in the book because they are rare imported kinds. In the beautiful Wyre Forest, for instance, there is a Whitty Pear, now rare but which was known hundreds of years ago. This particular species is from Italy and there is a theory that it was brought in by a Roman soldier during Roman Britain times. In the warmer southern parts of the country rare semi-tropical trees have been discovered. The great variety of species and the many local sub-species that you can meet will be enough to keep the budding expert busy for years.

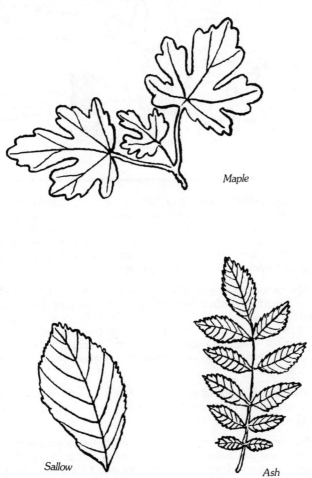

Maple

Sallow

Ash

16
Red Sky at Night

It is always sensible to make a check on the weather forecast before setting out, especially if you are walking in the hills or mountains. Television and radio forecasts are now quite accurate due to a greater use of modern technology, though the fiasco over the 1987 hurricane in Southern England is a reminder that they are by no means perfect. However, national forecasts cannot provide the degree of local detail that you need when conditions are varying rapidly.

The Meteorological Office provides local weather forecasts via the telephone with their 'Weathercall' service (numbers at the end of this chapter). These forecasts are updated three times a day. Remember, however, that they are charged at British Telecom's more expensive 'M' rate. Many of the National Parks also provide a weather service — especially valuable if you are walking in Snowdonia, the Lake District or other mountainous areas. It is worth making a note of numbers that you are likely to need.

But even with the national and local services it is useful to know a little about weather signs yourself since conditions can change quickly, and a little knowledge can sometimes be of great help.

Folklore can sometimes be useful: "Red sky at night, shepherd's delight Red sky in the morning, shepherd's warning" is a very old saying and, like many tales of this sort it is based on canny observations and experience. Like some ancient sayings it contains some degree of truth so we might keep our waterproofs handy if the morning sunrise is against a red sky, or expect a fine day if the sky has been red the night before.

124

When a halo is seen around the moon, another saying goes, there will be rain ahead. In fact there is usually rain within twenty-four hours. The halo occurs when clouds known as altostratus are around — these form a uniform grey sheet that blurs the image of the sun or moon. Altostratus are usually followed by lower and heavier rain clouds.

THE AMATEUR METEOROLOGIST

If you want to be a little more scientific there are three observations that you can make — barometric pressure, wind direction and cloud formation.

DEPRESSIONS

The atmosphere above us is in constant motion and our weather is largely determined by the behaviour of two principal air masses — cold air circulating over the north polar region and warm air circulating in the equatorial region. These masses rub against each other forming eddies — rather like the eddies that you will see where two streams meet. In the northern hemisphere these eddies circulate clockwise and so are said to be 'cyclonic'. They form regions of low pressure known as 'depressions' or 'lows'. Within the eddies cold polar air pushing down southward is called a 'cold front'; the corresponding movement of warm air is a 'warm front'.

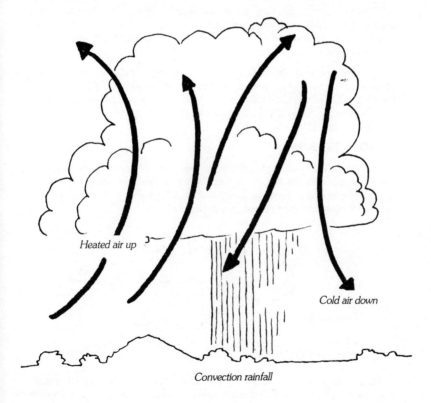

Heated air up

Cold air down

Convection rainfall

But, because nature abhors a vacuum, air tends to flow into the lows from the surrounding higher pressure areas known as 'anticyclones' or 'highs'. This results in winds blowing to the centres of the lows until these are filled up and the weather becomes more stable. It is the continual interplay of these highs and lows that gives rise to the great variability of the weather pattern in the British Isles. Other counties, it is said, have climate; in Britain we just have weather!

As a typical depression approaches, the barometric pressure gradually falls, a warm front passes across, followed eventually by a cold front. As the warm front meets colder air, clouds start to form, first high in the atmosphere, then lower down and bringing rain.

If the cold front is some way behind the warm front there may be a partial clearing of the weather. However, when it approaches, the wind will pick up and you can expect heavier rain. Following the cold front the sky can partly clear but with heavy cloud masses lurching through. These are rain clouds and the rain descending from them can often be seen from a distance. The bigger the clouds, the more vicious they can be, bringing rain, hail, thunder and heavy winds. If these approach then is the time to put on the waterproofs.

In practice, things may vary somewhat (weather cannot be relied on to behave according to rules!), but these main features will still be observed. If you study the weather carefully whenever you go walking you will eventually become proficient at recognising the warning signs.

You can recognise the passage of the depression by the behaviour of the barometer. A slow fall in pressure indicates a depression on its way. A rapid fall is a warning of lots of wind and rain squalls. A jump in pressure indicates that the cold front is passing through. If the pressure remains steady then the weather should remain unchanged.

WIND PATTERNS

Another indication of the likely weather behaviour can be obtained by observing the wind direction. As the atmosphere swirls around, the wind blowing on the ground may not be in the same direction as that high above. This can tell us where we are in relation to the passage of a depression.

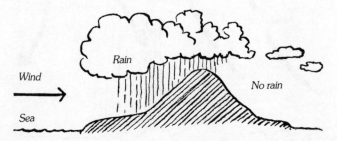

Stand with your back to the surface wind and look up to observe the direction of the clouds. If they come from the left then the weather will usually get worse in the next few hours; if the clouds come from the right there will usually be an improvement. A parallel movement of the clouds indicates not much change. When you do this be careful to get the true direction of the surface wind. Hills and mountains can distort the direction as the wind blows around them.

In the British Isles most of the wind streams reaching us come from the south-west where they have had a long journey over the ocean. Consequently they contain lots of moisture which they are inclined to discharge as soon as they reach a land mass. Mountains are particularly good at doing this which accounts for the fact that weather conditions there can be very different from surrounding lower lying areas.

Winds from the south-east have travelled over the continent so are dry and bring warm, usually cloudless, weather. They sometimes travel considerable distances and have, very occasionally, been known to bring Saharan sand with them — to the mystification of motorists who have found it deposited on their cars. South-easterly winds are, unfortunately, not very common in Britain.

North-easterly winds come from Siberia and Scandinavia. They bring cold, cloudy weather though, generally, not much rain.

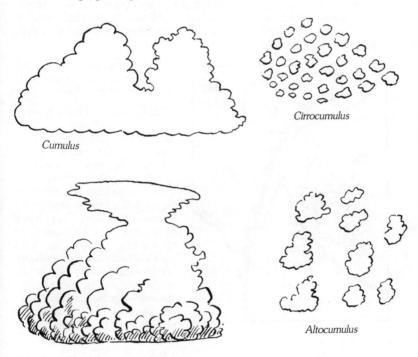

Cumulus

Cirrocumulus

Cumulonimbus

Altocumulus

127

North-westerly winds are rather less predictable. They may have come from polar regions bringing cold showers with them. Alternatively they may have originated in the south-west, passed over us, then been turned around by a depression to the north and returned. Usually they will have dropped their moisture the first time round so should give clear dry conditions.

CLOUDS

Clouds consist of masses of small water drops or ice crystals. They are formed by the condensation of water vapour in the atmosphere, usually by the cooling of upward moving streams of air. Cloud is usually classified as low (up to 10,000 feet), medium (10,000 to 25,000 feet), and high (25,000 to 35,000 feet). Cloud at ground level is mist or fog. The high clouds are composed of ice crystals, the lower ones of water droplets.

Clouds assume a great variety of shapes but fall generally into three categories. Cumulus are fat, 'cotton wool' type clouds typical of fair weather. Stratus clouds form as layers, and cirrus are fleecy clouds which form at great heights.

Each of these categories is sub-divided to give ten principal classes. For example, altocumulus clouds form between 6,500 and 20,000 feet. They are little flattened clouds which may be slightly grey in the middle with white edges.They are seen as groups or lines against a blue sky.

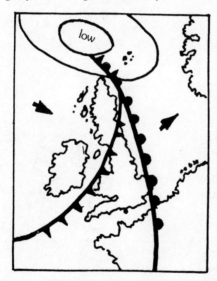

Wind flow
Warm front
Cold front
Occluded front

Clouds typify particular weather patterns and so can give valuable clues to the amateur forecaster.

Cirrus clouds commonly bring the first indication of an approaching warm front. These are high (up to 50,000 feet) and are of a delicate feathery appearance, sometimes called mare's tails. Cirrostratus will follow — this is the thin high cloud responsible for the halo around the sun or moon. It may be accompanied by patches of cirrocumulus — these are small cloudlets in flowing lines and often known as a mackerel sky. As the cirrostratus cuts off heat from the sun any earlier fair weather cumulus will disappear. At this stage you probably have two or three hours to prepare for rain.

When the warm front reaches you it wll be accompanied by dark grey nimbostratus. At this stage you should be wearing your waterproofs and be prepared for a period of steady rain or snow.

Beyond the warm front a cold front will be following, though before it arrives there may be a clearing of the skies. Typical of the cold front are cumulonimbus clouds which are heavy and voluminous, often with a typical anvil shape. These are often thunderstorm clouds, and as they approach you can often make out, below them, the dark diagonal lines of falling rain.

The air brought along by the cold front is often fresher and more invigorating than the moist warm air which preceded it. It may still bring some more showers but provides good conditions for walking.

A typical depression and its associated weather pattern is shown in the diagram — look out for these in the TV weather forecasts and in newspaper weather maps. The 'occluded front' is the section where the cold front has caught up with the warm front. The warm air rises and the cold air comes in underneath — this can often cause a lot of rain.

The centre of the depression usually follows a north-easterly track off the Hebrides. The southern part of Britain, being furthest from the centre, may then miss the worst of the bad weather. But not all depressions follow this track — if one comes along the English Channel this can bring lots of rain to the south.

Sometimes depressions follow zig-zag paths — this creates havoc with the forecasting!

Areas of low pressure are, of course, balanced somewhere by areas of high pressure (anticyclones). These usually bring fine weather, though much depends on where the anticyclone is centred and in which direction it is moving. Anticyclones move more slowly than depressions so a slowly rising barometer usually indicates that a high is approaching.

OTHER SIGNS

The behaviour of insects can sometimes give a clue to weather patterns. Midges and gnats swarmimg in the evening after rain indicate that a warm front has just passed. High flying insects indicate a high pressure anticyclone — these attract the attentions of swifts, swallows and martins so high flying flocks of these birds indicate settled conditions.

If the morning is misty, following a heavy dew, that is often a good sign. On the other hand a brassy bright sun in the morning seldom lasts throughout the day. Clear horizons where you can pick out distant features in sharp detail often indicate high winds ahead. The lingering trails from high flying aircraft is generally a bad sign, but if the trails quickly disappear this is usually an indication of settled conditions.

BUT ...

whatever the signs it is always sensible to be prepared for something worse. The only certainty about British weather is that you can never be certain of anything. If you really must have a guarantee of fine weather then you need to do your walking elsewhere — perhaps in the Sahara. But in that case you probably would not have read this book.

"I said 'Is this a force ten?'"

MET. OFFICE WEATHERCALL SERVICE

For regularly updated local weather forecasts dial 0898 500 followed by the regional code:

Greater London	401
Kent, Surrey & Sussex	402
Dorset, Hant. & IOW	403
Devon & Cornwall	404
Wiltshire, Glos., Avon & Somerset	405
Berks, Bucks & Oxfordshire	406
Beds, Herts & Essex	407
Norfolk, Suffolk & Cambridgeshire	408
West Midlands, S Glamorgan & Gwent	409
Shropshire, Hereford & Worcester	410
Central Midlands	411

A five-day National weather forecast can be obtained on 0898 500 430.

These calls are charged at the more expensive 'M' rate.

Appendix
Some useful addresses

Backpackers Club	20 St Michaels Road, Tilehurst, Reading RG3 4RP
British Mountaineering Council	Crawford House, Precinct Centre, Manchester University, Manchester M13 9RZ
Commons, Open Spaces and Footpath Preservation Society	25a Bell Street, Henley-on-Thames, Oxfordshire
Council for National Parks	45 Shelton Street, London WC2H 9HJ
Council for the Preservation of Rural England	4 Hobart Place, London SW1W 0HY
Council for the Preservation of Rural Wales	31 High Street, Powys
Countryside Commission	John Dower House, Crescent Place, Cheltenham, Gloucestershire GL50 3RA
Countryside Commission for Scotland	Battleby, Redgorton, Perth PH1 3EW
Countrywide Holidays	Birch Heys, Cromwell Range, Manchester M14 6HU
HF Holidays	142/144 Great North Way, London NW4 1EG
Long Distance Walkers Association	Lodgefield Cottage, High Street, Flimwell, Wadhurst, East Sussex
Mountaineering Council for Scotland	11 Kirklee Quadrant, Glasgow G12 0TS
National Trust	42 Queen Anne's Gate, London SW1H 9AS
National Trust for Scotland	5 Charlotte Square, Edinburgh EH2 4DU
Offa's Dyke Association	Old Primary School, West Street, Knighton, Powys LD7 1EW
Pennine Way Council	29 Springfield Park Avenue, Chelmsford, Essex CM2 6EL
Ramblers' Association	1/5 Wandsworth Road, London SW8 2XX
Ramblers Holidays	Box 43, Welwyn Garden City, Hertfordshire AL8 6PQ
Rare Breeds Survival Trust	4th Street, National Agricultural Centre, Kenilworth, Warwickshire CV8 2LG
Royal Society for Nature Conservation	The Green, Nettleham, Lincoln LN2 2NR

Scottish Rights of Way Society	28 Rutland Square, Edinburgh EH1 2BW
Scottish Youth Hostels Association	7 Glebe Crescent, Stirling FK8 2JA
Youth Hostels Association	Trevelyan House, St Albans, Hertfordshire AL1 2DY

Index

Notes

Notes

Notes

Notes